ARE YOU GOING TO A BETTER PLACE?

Richard R. Schmidt, D. Min., Ph.D.

Foreword By: Roman Claas

PROPHECY FOCUS MINISTRIES, INC.

www.ProphecyFocusMinistries.com

Editor in Chief: Mary Rebholz
Cover Design By: Valori L. Schmidt

Are You Going to a Better Place?

ISBN-13: 9798428551181

Prophecy Focus Ministries
P.O. Box 122
Hales, Corners, WI 53130
www.ProphecyFocusMinistries.com

Prophecy Focus Ministries, Inc. is recognized by the Internal Revenue Service as a **501(c)(3)** corporation. This book is designed to advance transformational research in Biblical/theological education.

Printed in the **United States of America**

Are You Going to "A Better Place?"

CONTENTS

DEDICATION

This book is dedicated first to all of the people I worked with while a sworn member of the Milwaukee County Sheriff's Office. I often stated in various venues that "I love" the people I worked with and had the privilege to lead for a season. May this short work help you understand how I could sincerely love each person, even if we embrace different political positions or personal ideologies.

This book is also dedicated to the many elected officials and civil servants that fight for the values and truths they hold dear. This is for Democrats, Republicans, Libertarians, Independents, Socialists, and all others who embrace a political ideology. I humbly ask for one chance to share with you the most important event in history that could literally change your life, as it did mine. And no, it has nothing to do with politics.

This book is dedicated to every person of every race, ethnic origin, skin color, gender, creed, and any other defining characteristic that makes you a unique person. Society and cultural norms take great pains to make many people and people groups feel devalued, unloved, and rejected. For a few moments, you, yes you, are all that matters. You will find something here that seems so foreign to so many, that God uniquely loves you as an individual person. YOU will be shown how you can receive a special, priceless gift that is waiting for YOU.

YOU may have arrived at the very top of your profession. You may have wealth, fame, and achieved what others only dream they could accomplish. You feel highly valued, and maybe even loved by the masses. This book is also dedicated to you, because the ultimate gift, if you have not already received it, waits for YOU.

This book is for YOU.

YOU matter more than YOU may have ever imagined.

FOREWORD by ROMAN H. CLAAS

This workbook should be a must read for everyone who has reached the age of reason. There are people who answer this question, "Are you going to a better place?" by stating "I hope so", and then there are those who thought they answered the question a long time ago by stating, "yes, I'm going to heaven", but now are having second thoughts. Then, there are those who've known for some time that they are going to a better place for sure.

In this workbook, you play the role of victim, jury, and judge, and you are presented with indisputable and undeniable facts along the way, to help you come up with the right answers and ultimately the verdict you need.

The author, my longtime friend Rich Schmidt, knows Scripture, and when he speaks, you need to listen. When he writes, you need to read. Let him walk you thru the steps to make a decision based on the facts found in God's Word. Three things are for certain: 1. We are all going to die; 2. We will spend eternity in hell; or, 3. We will spend eternity in heaven.

Why gamble with your eternal future? Read this book, and then make the right decision.

PREFACE

You are personally invited into the courtroom where you are the defendant, jury, and judge. The scenario presented is not speculation, but a reality that you are actually living. The evidence found in this book is undeniable, and there is zero room for speculation or tainting of the facts. You have no option but to make a judicial determination that will literally affect not only your present situation, but also the place where you will spend eternity.

Humanity, from a cultural perspective, is conditioned to reject statements of fact, and to look at everything through the eyes of relativism, especially when it involves religion and faith. Doctors practice medicine. Attorneys practice law. Professionals spend years in schools of higher education attempting to learn the facts that will give them successful careers. Tradespeople spend concentrated time learning their craft to produce the best possible results. Every person spends time studying, starting from childhood, to prepare them to function in society and have the best chance to succeed in life.

When it comes to "religion," people often make decisions based on hearsay and what seems to make sense or pleases the emotional need for the moment. We tend to listen to what our parents or some religious person stated and take it as truth without question. We are prone to dismiss what is suggested as the essential, absolute, necessity of determining our eternal destiny based on fact, and not mere speculation.

How long will you live: 20, 40, 60, 80, 100 years? And then you will enter eternity where you will be very conscious for the next 2,000, 10,000, 10-billion years, yes eternity. Our finite minds cannot understand a timeless eternity. However, just because the concept is beyond our human comprehension does not make it any less true.

The ultimate reminder of the reality of breathing one's final breath is a funeral. The people gather and many times attempt to console each other by stating, "They are in a better place." How do you know they are in "a better place"? For you personally, how do you know if you will one day be in "a better place"? Have you obtained documented, verifiable evidence that guarantees your "better place" scenario? Is there verifiable evidence that you could be in a far worse place? Remember, that the very premise of this book starts with the absolute, verifiable fact that you, yes you, are deeply loved by God beyond what you may currently comprehend. However, that love does not negate the fact that God is also just. The Scriptures contain the one way that God's justice can be satisfied, guaranteeing you, the defendant, an eternal dwelling place with Him. There is no guess work involved. The evidence is undeniable and overwhelming, and will be presented in this book.

This book will provide you, in the pages that follow, hundreds of verifiable facts that will allow you, the defendant, to provide an intelligent verdict on your present situation and eternal destination. In a short book like this that may seem impossible. The following pages will document hundreds of undeniable facts that were revealed weeks to thousands of years before they actually occurred with 100% accuracy.

Politics, government, and daily life are always subject to change with unintended consequences. For years I have stressed this fact: "Government does not change the heart, only God can change and transform the heart." This leads us to the point at which we are ready to start examining the documented facts that will push you to make a decision regarding not only your daily life, but your eternal destiny.

I will share how I personally came to a place of decision regarding the evidence presented to me when a teenager, and then we will examine the plethora of documented evidence that you the defendant, jury, and judge will use to determine your verdict and eternal sentence. The evidence that this book presents is not man-made rhetoric, creeds, confessions, or liturgy. The very Words of God, as preserved in the inerrant, and infallible Scriptures, contain the evidence that you will examine. Please do not gloss over this fact and think that because you went to a particular church, or took a sacrament as a baby, child, or adult that your destination is guaranteed. This is potentially the most serious book you will ever read, with the exception of the Scriptures, that will demand your honest, truthful verdict.

The Lord allowed me to spend 32 wonderful years in the Milwaukee County Sheriff's Office. I had the privilege of serving in many a courtroom and providing testimony in hundreds of cases. The judge's main purpose in every hearing and trial was to do everything within the bounds of the rule of law to get to the truth. There were rare times when the jury and judge got it wrong. On occasion, the facts became skewed by excellent speeches and rhetoric. The innocent actually became the guilty in the system that was designed to protect them.

A wrong verdict is an intolerable and unacceptable result. This book will not employ rhetoric, or well-orchestrated speeches, although I will provide my personal testimony of what changed my life. We will then move beyond my account, and strictly provide the undeniable, documented facts that will take you the defendant, and allow you to determine as the jury and judge not only your verdict, but your eternal sentence. I look forward to hearing from you. If you have questions, or this small book leads you to make a judicial determination in your life, my contact information is available on the back cover of this book.

Are YOU Going to a Better Place?

CHAPTER 1
EVIDENCE OF A CHANGED LIFE!

Please allow me the latitude to share my personal testimonial with you. My parents provided a very loving home. My dad worked outside the home, and mom stayed home working tirelessly to care for me and my two sisters. Mom and dad were both conservative in their worldview, and they believed in following what could be described as a Biblical set of ethics and morals. They both were very faithful in making sure that I went to church and Sunday school every week, which I actually enjoyed for the most part. I vividly remember my mother making sure I had on a nice wool suit when I was a little boy. She would painstakingly iron my starched shirt, and make sure my pants and coat were in pristine condition. Dad would carefully put on my clip-on tie, make sure my shoes were polished, so that we looked our best when going to church. My parents had the belief that one should desire to look their best when going to church, as a sign of respect to God. Later in life, I would come to grips with the fact that God was not necessarily impressed with how I looked, but He was very concerned about my personal relationship with Him.

I always thought highly of the Bible and religion, even from my earliest memories, but I never had an assurance of where I would go if I were to die. I spent many years in Sunday school, listening to sermons from pastors, and trying to determine exactly what I needed to do to one day go to heaven. No one seemed to provide me with an explanation that guaranteed me an assurance of going to heaven. In fact, those I respected seemed only to guarantee that there was not a guarantee that heaven would be my home after my death.

My mother had multiple ailments her entire life. Several of her internal organs were removed in what today are fairly routine surgeries, but back in her day, they were much more invasive procedures. My little mind, as a young boy, was terrified every time mom would enter the hospital for surgery. I was sincerely scared that my precious, loving mother would die, and my heart could not handle that potential consequence.

One time shortly before my mom was scheduled to go into the hospital, I vividly recall asking her for something small of hers that I could keep with me every moment of the day and night to keep her figuratively close to me. She tenderly gave me a very beautiful lace handkerchief, which I tucked safely in my clothes 24 hours a day. The handkerchief represented my mother, and when she went into the hospital, that simple piece of cloth was my only lifeline to my mom. The thought of my dear mother dying was heart wrenching. I needed help. I needed comfort. I needed to have answers about what happens at death.

Where does one go to get answers about death, especially a young boy? Most people who want answers to the questions surrounding death go to a parent, friend, someone they know who is religious, maybe a television program, a religious radio show or an internet site, and of course the old standby in every neighborhood, the local church. As a young boy, I talked to my dad and grandmother regarding their perspective on death and eternity. I also talked to my Sunday school teacher and pastor, but no one, not one single person, was able to provide me with undeniable, documented facts concerning death, and what happens after that terrifying event.

The people I consulted threw out some ideas, a few contextually inappropriate verses from the Bible, but not one of them, including the pastor, provided me with what I would later as a teenager come to know as the gospel. The gospel, or in the original Greek of the New Testament, *euangelion*, is the documented, undeniable record of exactly how one can know for sure that heaven will be their eternal home.

Unfortunately, for years, I would go without the question of my eternal destination answered from a factual point of view. I heard many stories and messages about how I should attempt to live my life. There was a great deal of talk about helping and loving people, and doing things that were pleasing and non-offensive to others. But literally, there was nothing that gave me an assurance of where I would go when, not if, I would die. Everything was based on what I did or did not do, and no teacher, preacher, priest, or religious leader provided any irrefutable, documented evidence to guarantee me a place in heaven after death. Can you relate to this dilemma?

I grew up with two sisters, one older and one younger. Again, I was brought up in a wonderful, loving home, a home where church and God were honored; and my parents set a reasonable but firm set of moral and ethical rules that we the children were expected to follow. But there were certain pieces of the eternal puzzle that were missing. How much "good" was good enough to get into heaven? Where was the specific list of things to do? What happens if one missed something on the list? Was there any remedy if one did something wrong? Was there any possible way to reach a secure verdict on where one will spend eternity?

When I was a sophomore in high school, my older sister came home one afternoon after attending some function. I had no idea what she had attended, but something radically changed. She began to act very different toward me. Like most siblings, we got along at times, but my older sister and I often had conflicts and verbal fights. However, on a particular day, when she came home, she just seemed different. I had no idea why she was acting in what I could only describe at the time as a strange manner. I watched her carefully over the next few weeks because she was treating me differently, much differently than she had ever treated me before.

Instead of her being antagonistic and even at times caustic toward me, she suddenly was acting in a loving and caring manner. Her demeanor definitely got my attention.

Finally, after several weeks of her still maintaining a more pleasant demeanor toward me than in the past, I got angry with her. I came up to her, got in her face and said, "Listen, why in the world are you treating me nicely? What do you want? What are you trying to get from me?" I found her being nice more annoying than when she was exercising her old personality of being antagonistic.

My sister acknowledged she was acting different, but she could not verbalize what had taken place in her life that changed her attitude toward me and others. The only thing she said to me were three little, but powerful words, "Come and see," which I would later find out came directly from the Bible, from a very similar scenario.

My sister informed me that after high school classes were completed for the day, there was a Bible study that took place in a lady's home across the street from the high school. She further informed me that there were many young people our age that met at the home, and it was there that she heard something totally different than she had ever heard before.

The inquisitive side of me wanted to know why my sister had a dramatic change in her life. I determined that I was going to go to that lady's home and hear what she had to say. After school one day, I walked across the street to the house where my sister had directed me to go. A wonderful, kind lady met me at the entrance of the house and I saw many teenagers in her home. The group was sitting around the living room and having what appeared to be a very pleasant time. Many were talking about religious things, and a few were singing together. This was an interesting scenario, but I watched and attempted to digest what was taking place around me.

The middle-aged lady began a more structured time of singing and a subsequent Bible lesson. It was there for the first time, after being in church all my life, that I heard something that I had never heard before. The leader gave a message which was astounding new material to me. I had attended church for some 16 years straight, and never once had I heard what this speaker presented that day. It was at this simple home Bible study that I believe I heard for the very first time the Biblical account of the gospel. The speaker provided the four key points of the gospel message to the group straight from the Bible.

As I would learn, the gospel is absolute truth taken completely from the Bible, God's Word. The Biblical gospel is not a creed, a man-made confession, or liturgy. The gospel did not come from human origin, but directly from God, as recorded in the Scriptures.

The theological defense of the Bible as the very Word of God is known as apologetics. In this short work, the massive amount of material that backs up the Bible as God's Word will not be presented, except in a short summary form. There are many excellent books on apologetics, for example, Josh McDowell's works present scholarly and extremely well documented material on the subject.[1]

When the leader began sharing, what I heard for the very first time was four key elements from the Bible, that comprise the gospel. The first element of the gospel is that every person is a sinner. The speaker shared from Romans 3:10, that "there is none righteous, no not one." Then she moved to Romans 3:23, "all have sinned and come short of the glory of God." I had no problem accepting that fact. I knew I wasn't perfect, which is one of the reasons why I had been searching for documented truth on how anyone could know for sure that when they died, they indeed would go to a better place known as heaven.

The second element of the gospel that the leader shared was that because everyone was a sinner, if they got what they truly deserved, they would spend an eternity in an awful place called the lake of fire (Revelation 21:8), or to use a very politically incorrect term, hell. She turned in her Bible to Romans 6:23, which states that "the wages of sin is death, but the gift of God is eternal life in Christ Jesus our Lord." I already knew that everyone was going to die one day, so again, this was not a new revelation. She made it very clear, and firmly stressed that the wages, specifically what one earned because of their sin, was death. In other words, death was the reasonable payment for sin.

I stood in the exact same place I had stood all my life. I'm a sinner, condemned because of my failure to be perfect. It got worse. Not only was death referring to physical death, but also (according to the Bible) the second or spiritual death, which results in eternal separation from God in the lake of fire. Revelation 21:8 states, "But the cowardly, unbelieving, abominable, murderers, sexually immoral, sorcerers, idolaters, and all liars shall have their part in the lake which burns with fire and brimstone, which is the second death." This verse lists what some may consider major sins, but ends with a sin that virtually everyone would have to admit to, lying. That one little transgression of lying validates the first point of the gospel that every person is indeed a sinner.

---

[1] Josh McDowell, *The New Evidence that Demands a Verdict* (Nashville TN.: Thomas Nelson, Inc) 1999.

Is there any hope of "going to a better place" when one dies? Is there any possible way to avoid the penalty for sin, eternal separation from God in the lake of fire? Does documented, verifiable evidence exist that one could know beyond a reasonable doubt that heaven will be their eternal home?

The third element in the gospel presentation lead me closer to the answers. The leader turned in her Bible to several passages describing what Jesus Christ had personally done to pay the sin debt, which was on every human being's personal account.

God created Adam, the first person on earth sinless (Genesis 1-2). God specifically commanded Adam, before He created Eve, not to eat from the tree of the knowledge of good and evil. However, in short order, Eve and subsequently Adam, succumbed to the temptation of Satan, and ate the one thing that God specifically commanded they should not eat, which was fruit from the tree named "the knowledge of good and evil." Genesis 2:15–17 states, "Then the LORD God took the man [Adam] and put him in the garden of Eden to tend and keep it. And the LORD God commanded the man, saying, 'Of every tree of the garden you may freely eat; but of the tree of the knowledge of good and evil you shall not eat, for in the day that you eat of it you shall surely die.'"

Shortly after God gave the command to Adam not to eat from the forbidden tree, God created another perfect, sinless person named Eve (Genesis 2:21-25). God brought Adam and Eve together and instituted the first marriage. However, tragedy would very quickly strike, resulting in the curse of sin and death being passed to every single descendent of Adam and Eve, which includes everyone, past, present, and future, as absolutely every person is related by blood to Adam and Eve.

Genesis chapter 3 documents the temptation of Adam and Eve, and the unfortunate truth that both ate from the forbidden tree. The fact is, neither Adam nor Eve would have ever died if they would not have disobeyed the rule of law and ate from the forbidden tree. It is that simple. When Adam ate the fruit, physical and spiritual death became a reality (Genesis 3:19). You and I stand condemned before God, the defendants of what Adam specifically did, when he willfully disobeyed his Creator.

The New Testament documents that the physical father transfers the sin nature to his children, based upon the first sinful act of

Adam when he disobeyed God and ate from the forbidden tree of the knowledge of good and evil. Romans 5:12 states, "Therefore, just as through one man [Adam] sin entered the world, and death through sin, and thus death spread to all men, because all sinned." In other words, every single person who has a human father, which of course is everyone except Jesus, received the sinful nature. The speaker provided the documented evidence that would unequivocally substantiate the truth of what Jesus accomplished on behalf of sinful humanity. Jesus Christ, God Himself, a member of the Trinity consisting of God the Father, the Son, and the Holy Spirit (Matthew 28:19-20), literally left the glory of heaven to come to the earth in human form. The Scriptures clearly state that Jesus was virgin born (Isaiah 7:14; Matthew 1:22-23). Why does it matter that Jesus was born of a virgin? The documented reason Jesus absolutely had to be virgin born was because the Scriptures identify the father as the vessel through whom the sin nature is transferred to their child. These statements mandate a close look at the verifiable evidence.

This is a key piece of evidence that Jesus had to be born of a virgin (Isaiah 7:14), otherwise He would have had the sin nature, and therefore be unable to make the complete payment demanded by God for the debt for sin. Only the sinless Savior, Jesus Christ could satisfy the judicial demand of God Himself. The Scripture clearly states that Jesus was tempted in all ways just as any other human being, yet He never transgressed the law of God. Hebrews 4:14–15 reveals, "Seeing then that we have a great High Priest who has passed through the heavens, Jesus the Son of God, let us hold fast our confession. For we do not have a High Priest who cannot sympathize with our weaknesses, but was in all points tempted as we are, yet without sin."

Jesus absolutely could not save human beings from their sins if He had a physical human father that inseminated Mary, the mother of Jesus. Therefore, the Holy Spirit came down upon Mary, and placed the baby Jesus into Mary's womb (Matthew 1:18-21). And then, after Mary went through the process of a normal pregnancy, the Lord Jesus Christ was born, born of the virgin Mary, an absolute necessity for the ability to pay the penalty for sin.

Jesus Christ's birth is not what took away the penalty for sin. The Lord Jesus spent some thirty-three years on this earth. The Bible documents many of the teachings and miracles of Jesus, substantiating the fact that He was indeed God. Jesus would in fact, perform the one and only act that would satisfy the justice of the righteous God. The only act that could remove the penalty for sin was the crucifixion of Jesus, which is where the entire gospel account becomes reality.

Why would Jesus Christ, God's Son, go to a cross and willingly give His life? Why would God Himself take on the form of a human being, live some thirty-three years in a natural body, and then suddenly allow Himself to be arrested, and falsely condemned to the most horrible possible death known to man at that time, crucifixion? The answer is very simple.

Have you ever seen John 3:16 written on a billboard, wall, sidewalk, barn, sign, subway, or elsewhere? Carefully read the judicial promise that God provides for you in the passage. "For God so loved the world, [each one of us], that He gave His only begotten Son, [Jesus Christ], that whosoever believeth in Him, [anyone who would believe in Him in His death, His burial and His resurrection] should not perish [or go to an eternity in the lake of fire], but have everlasting life." John 3:17, the very next verse, spells out in more detail why Jesus Christ went to the cross. "For God did not send His Son into the world to condemn the world, but that the world through Him might be saved." The word *saved* in Scripture has a strong theological meaning. *Saved* in the Biblical context, refers to one being completely delivered from, or *saved* from the penalty of sin.[2] Saved is a judicial determination made by God alone.

Let us rehearse one more time Revelation 21:8. The verse provides us with a list of what many of us would call very severe sins. "But the cowardly, unbelieving, abominable, murderers, sexually immoral, sorcerers, idolaters, and all liars shall have their part in the lake which burns with fire and brimstone, which is the second death."

---

[2] William Arndt et al., *A Greek-English Lexicon of the New Testament and Other Early Christian Literature* (Chicago: University of Chicago Press, 2000), 982.

Pay attention to the word *liars*. Can I ask you a personal question? Have you ever told a lie? I have never met a person on this earth yet, who will honestly state that they have never told a lie? One lie marks a person as a liar. God is very aware when one sins, and God holds everyone accountable for the sin of lying, as every other sin committed, and places it on your record. And what does the law, the documentation, state that one deserves for being a liar? The law states, regarding those that have lied, that God has the judicial right to sentence them to the lake which burns with fire and brimstone, which is the second death. You may determine that the law is unfair. You may personally refuse to accept that judicial determination. You may want to go to a court of appeals, but no such court exists. However, there is an absolute, documented way to have your sinful record completed expunged, without the ability to ever appear again. The Judge has provided the one and only way for you to clearly go "to a better place," known as heaven.

This leads us to the question, and the title of the book, are you truly going to "a better place"? According to Revelation 21:8, if we received what we judicially deserve, we would not be going to a better place, but a horrible, devastating, catastrophic place, known as the eternal lake of fire, which is the called "the second death." This is not God's desire for you, and God has provided the exclusive remedy.

The good news is still awaiting. We are currently in a world of hurt based on the current evidence. The Scriptures, the rule of law, unequivocally state that all individuals are sinners. The second undeniable judicial determination is that the penalty of sin is the eternal lake of fire. The third element of the gospel is the good news that Jesus Christ, God's son, loved you so much, that he came down from heaven, and died on the cross as the only judicially approved complete payment for your sins. Jesus not only died, but He was buried. Why was He buried? Why would he stay in the grave three days? It was to prove, beyond a shadow of a doubt, that He died. It's no mystery. There is no getting around it. Jesus Christ physically died.

It is imperative that we examine the judicial evidence found in First Corinthians 15:3-4. The apostle Paul records, "For I delivered to you first of all that which I also received: that Christ died for our sins according to the Scriptures, and that He was buried, and that He rose again the third day according to the Scriptures."

These verses provide the three specific things Jesus accomplished to provide payment for sin. The gospel includes that Jesus not only died and was buried, but He most importantly rose from the dead, proving that he indeed was God, as the only One who could satisfy the righteous Judge.

The Gospel means the good news, the *euangelion*. Now is the time to examine the fourth element to the gospel, which many people unfortunately miss as I did, until the speaker at the home Bible study brought the following undeniable fact to my attention.

You may rightly have concluded that you are in complete agreement with the facts presented up to this point. You may have already accepted that you are a sinner. You already knew that because you sinned you do not deserve to go to heaven. You may also believe that Jesus Christ died on the cross, was buried, and three days later rose from the grave.

Now comes the operative issue. The first three elements of the gospel message, give you the facts. It is the same concept as believing that a president that you have never met existed. It is simply believing that historical events have taken place, such as wars, conflicts, elections, and inventions. Believing an historical account is a choice, but believing does not necessarily change who you are.

The fourth and final major element of the gospel message is the one elusive, yet documented point that so often one misses in the evidentiary chain. Let us go back to the well-known verse, John 3:16. Grasp and embrace the personal promise that the verse expresses. "For God, so loved the world *(put your name in this place)* that He *God* gave His only begotten Son, [the death, burial and resurrection of Jesus Christ] that whosoever *(put your name in this place)* believes in Him [In Jesus-His death, burial and resurrection] should not perish [Go to the eternal lake of fire/hell] but have everlasting life [Eternal life in heaven in the presence of the Lord].

The Scriptures contain a much more detailed set of verses that are not as well known, but they expand on the evidence already presented with a very specific explanation of what precisely you need to accept, to absolutely guarantee that you will go to "a better place" known as heaven. Ephesians 2:8-9 provide the documented answer regarding how to guarantee you will have eternal life with the Lord Jesus. "For by grace are you saved through faith, and that not of yourselves; it is the gift of God, not of works, lest anyone should boast."

As with any law, it is imperative to understand the author's intent and meaning. Words matter, and each word and phrase contain a very specific meaning that provides the perfect, absolute, unequivocal evidence required for one to obtain eternal life in "a better place," heaven.

What is the meaning of the phrase, "For by grace?" Grace is a free, unmerited gift.[3] Grace can be likened to a person showing up at an event or party, and some unknown person walks up to them and hands them a priceless gift. The recipient did nothing to receive the gift. It was undeserved and unearned.

For by grace, "are you saved." What does the word *saved* mean? The word carries the judicial weight of complete deliverance from the penalty of sin.[4] Romans 6:23 documented the wages of sin is death. Revelation 21:8 provided undeniable evidence that the penalty of sin is the second death, synonymous with spiritual death, which is eternity in the lake of fire. God makes the judicial determination that when He declares a person saved, they are set free from the penalty for sin.

For by grace, are you saved "through faith." What is faith? Hebrews 11:1 defines Biblical faith this way, "Now faith is the substance of things hoped for, the evidence of things not seen." The fact is, not even one of us will experience Jesus coming down from heaven, looking us directly in our face, and telling us that we must believe in Him. Not

---

[3] William Arndt et al., *A Greek-English Lexicon of the New Testament and Other Early Christian Literature* (Chicago: University of Chicago Press, 2000), 982.
[4] Ceslas Spicq and James D. Ernest, *Theological Lexicon of the New Testament* (Peabody, MA: Hendrickson Publishers, 1994), 345.

one of us will have Jesus tap us on the shoulder and say, "Listen, I want to tell you how to get to heaven."

Maybe you question why God does not make a personal appearance to you. God made the judicial determination that you can only obtain the free undeserved gift of eternal life through faith. It is believing by faith alone in what Jesus accomplished through His death, burial, and resurrection. The faith God demands, and explains in His rule of law, the Scriptures, can be likened to the faith you exercise when you read and believe that Abraham Lincoln was an actual person. It is the belief for the younger reader that Martin Luther King existed, even though you never physically saw him. It is by faith because you have not seen it. You have read historical stated facts in books. You have heard lectures from individuals claiming to provide historical facts. The Scriptures state, "For by grace," God's free, unmerited gift, "are you saved" from the penalty of sin through faith alone.

For by grace, are you saved through faith "and that not of yourself." This is a very crucial piece of evidence. There is absolutely nothing you can do to earn eternal life in heaven. This is the major issue that virtually everyone faces based on what they personally believe about the way to earn a place in heaven. This verse absolutely obliterates the unbiblical thought that one's personal good works have the ability to deliver them from the penalty of sin. No one will get to heaven, no one will avoid the penalty of hell, by anything they have done. God's documented gospel plan mandates that He can only declare one free from the penalty of sin when one places their faith in what Jesus accomplished in His death, burial, and resurrection.

For by grace, are you saved through faith, it is not of yourselves, "it is the gift of God." Now let us go to Christmas time or a birthday party, or a special event where someone took some time and they picked out a gift for you. How do you receive that gift? You receive that gift by simply reaching out and letting them place that gift in your hands, or maybe they placed it on the floor underneath a Christmas tree or in a special place, and you see the gift that is there for you. You simply reach out and take the gift. You embrace it, you open it, and you keep it as a gift. You paid nothing for the gift. You simply reached out and took the gift and made it your own. And that is exactly what God states is the only way to guarantee you will one day go to "a better place"; it is by accepting the undeserved free gift of eternal life.

For by grace, are you saved through faith, and that not of yourselves, it is the gift of God, "not of works." Did you catch that? Every single religion teaches that one receives deliverance from the penalty of wrongdoing, and earns a place in heaven, paradise, or other positive place based solely upon the good things that they accomplish. Most people when asked if they will go to heaven when they die state that they hope they will get to heaven. Many answer that they have tried to live a good life, and they trust that God will see them as having accomplished more good works than bad.

For by grace, are you saved through faith, and that not of yourselves, it is the gift of God, not of works, "lest anyone should boast." God adds a specific, intentional qualifier to these two verses. Why is God not interested in your good works when it comes to obtaining an eternal place in heaven? God is not interested in what one does, which is boasting about one's own accomplishments. What God the Father is interested in hearing is that one acknowledges that His Son, the Lord Jesus Christ, left heaven's glory, took on the form of a humble human, and literally suffered as no person ever suffered and died to judicially pay for one's sin. No one did anything to merit in the eyes of a righteous God a place in heaven. Jesus, through His death, burial and resurrection provided the only remedy for sin. Ephesians 2:8-9 provides the absolute rule of law on how one goes to "a better place" known as heaven. It is through faith alone in what the Lord Jesus accomplished.

Let me provide a little illustration. Imagine that you have a son, a daughter, or someone that you love dearly who placed their own life in jeopardy to save another person. For example, say your loved one was walking along the street when they encountered a person robbing a stranger at gunpoint and threatening to kill that person. Your son, daughter, or loved one yelled at the person with the gun and ordered the offender to leave the person alone. Your loved one became completely engaged in the deadly scenario and attempted to save the life of the stranger as they pushed the gunman away. The gunman screamed, "get out of the way or I will kill you!" Your precious loved one stood their ground. The gunman shot and killed your son, daughter or precious loved one. Your loved one fell dead, while the other person escaped.

Somehow you find out who the person was whose life your loved one saved. You go to that person's home and want to meet the person that your loved one sacrificed their life to save. Imagine your horror when the person who was able to run away based on the sacrifice of your loved one states, "Your loved one did nothing for me. I did it all myself. I ran away. I fled. I saved my own life. The death of your loved one is on him/her. That is not my problem. I can tell you again what I did to save myself. Get it right, your loved one's death did nothing to save me." How would you feel? God Himself looked down at his Son and watched Him as He suffered, bled, and died. Jesus Christ sacrificed His life to pay for your sin. Therefore, God makes it crystal clear that your good works are meaningless when it comes to the payment for your sin debt.

What does the rule of law, the Scriptures mandate?

But when the kindness and the love of God our Savior toward man appeared, *not by works of righteousness which we have done*, but according to His mercy He saved us, through the washing of regeneration and renewing of the Holy Spirit, whom He poured out on us abundantly through Jesus Christ our Savior, that having been justified by His grace we should become heirs according to the hope of eternal life (Titus 3:4–7).

But that *no one is justified by the law in the sight of God* is evident, for "the just shall live by faith." Yet the law is not of faith, but "the man who does them shall live by them." Christ has redeemed us from the curse of the law, having become a curse for us (for it is written, "Cursed is everyone who hangs on a tree"), that the blessing of Abraham might come upon the Gentiles in Christ Jesus, that *we might receive the promise of the Spirit through faith* (Galatians 3:11–14).

For by grace you have been saved through faith, and that *not of yourselves*; it is the gift of God, *not of works*, lest anyone should boast (Ephesians 2:8–9).

I listened intently at the Bible study, and things started to make sense. I was taught my entire life that my chance of going to heaven depended completely on the good works I performed. Now, the evidence presented at the Bible study provided a completely different set of verifiable, documented facts. Though at the time I had no idea there were thousands of Bible believing churches that taught the Biblical way to heaven, at this point in my life, maybe like you, I had never gone to a church that taught strictly the truths as revealed in the Bible.

I very carefully thought through the evidence provided in the Scriptures over the next two weeks. Finally, after reading the Bible for hours, and carefully examining the evidence, I turned from being the victim of Adam's original sin, and accepted the free gift of eternal life. I received God's free gift that He provides when one places their faith alone in the work Jesus Christ Himself accomplished through His death, burial, and resurrection. I vividly remember going into the basement of my parent's home, kneeling by a studio couch, and praying to the Lord. I told the Lord that I knew I was a sinner, deserving of eternal punishment. I now understood that I could not earn heaven. I continued, "I now accept the free gift of eternal life and am placing my faith in what Jesus, Your Son, did through His death, burial, and resurrection, in paying completely the penalty for my sin. Thank you for saving me from the penalty of sin and promising to take me to heaven when I die. In Jesus name, amen." At the time, I had no idea that I was praying what many refer to in Bible believing churches as the sinner's prayer. The prayer is not what brings salvation, but the faith placed in Jesus Christ certainly does, as the evidence has shown. The prayer simply related what had already taken place in the exercise of placing faith in the Lord Jesus.

In essence, the jury, made up of one person, carefully deliberated over the evidence. The jury then approached the judge, yes, myself, and the jury determined that I was guilty of being a sinner, deserving eternal life in hell. However, based upon my acceptance of the free gift of eternal life through placing my faith in Jesus Christ, and accepting His complete payment for my sin through His death, burial, and resurrection, I now after taking my last breath, would immediately go directly to heaven. The judge accepted the jury's verdict, and declared the person on trial free from the penalty of sin, and now free to go to heaven when life on this earth ended.

The Bible states that for Christians, defined as those who accept the free gift of eternal life, when they die, they are absent from the body and immediately present with the Lord (2 Corinthians 5:8). There is no future judgment after death for the true believer in Jesus Christ. It is literally death, and an immediate transfer of the person to the presence of Jesus Christ. This is the evidence that demands your personal deliberation. The rest of this short book will expand upon the evidence, and if you have not already accepted the gift of eternal life, I trust the documentation will provide the judicial proof needed to personally accept the gift God so graciously wants to give you.

CHAPTER 2
Evidence that Demands Your Verdict
One-Thousand Documented Reasons Why The Bible
Should Get Your Attention

The question that many of you are asking right now is, where are you going to find 1,000 literal documented reasons proving that the Bible is indeed the very Word of God. Dr. John Walvoord, former president of Dallas Theological Seminary, one of the premier seminaries in our country, wrote a book entitled *Every Prophecy of the Bible*.[5] In that outstanding work, Dr. Walvoord pointed out that there were 1,000 prophecies in the Bible when originally written. The Bible was written over a 1500-year period, by 40 inspired authors, on three different continents (Africa, Europe, and Asia). The inspired authors wrote the Bible's original manuscripts in three different languages: the Old Testament in Hebrew and a small portion in Aramaic, and the entire New Testament in Koine Greek. The church fathers compiled the sixty-six books into what now most people have in their homes, the Bible, the very Word of God.

Dr. Walvoord documents that of those 1,000 detailed, specific prophecies (predictions of the future), 500 of them have already occurred exactly as written.[6] Many of those 500 prophecies were written hundreds of years before they were fulfilled. The Bible clearly states that even one prophetic error is unacceptable, and any person who uttered a prophesy that did not come true received the death penalty.

> But the prophet who presumes to speak a word in My name, which I have not commanded him to speak, or who speaks in the name of other gods, that prophet shall die.' And if you say in your heart, 'How shall we know the word which the LORD has not spoken?'—when a prophet speaks in the name of the LORD,

---

[5] John Walvoord, *Every Prophecy of the Bible* (Colorado Springs, CO: Chariot Victor Publishing) 1999.
[6] Walvoord, 7.

if the thing does not happen or come to pass, that is the thing which the LORD has not spoken; the prophet has spoken it presumptuously; you shall not be afraid of him. (Deuteronomy 18:20–22)

God allows a zero rate of error in His perfect Word. Inerrancy dictates that every single prophecy must be fulfilled exactly as written. There are 351 specific prophecies regarding the advent, or first coming of Jesus Christ to the earth. Appendix A, at the end of this book, contains the complete list of those prophecies, including the address (chapter and verse) of the original prophecy and the address that documents its fulfillment. Attempting to determine the statistical probability of all 351 prophecies literally coming to a precise fulfillment is more zeros than we can count. No other "religious" book in the history of the world has ever provided documentation of hundreds of accurately fulfilled prophecies. This truth is way beyond a casual fact. The documentation provides detailed evidence, and undeniable historical facts. Are you going to "a better place" when you die? What evidence are you trusting with your answer? Eternal life in heaven or hell should not be open to speculation, unproven statements, or one's feelings or experiences. This eternal issue demands documented, verifiable evidence, which only the Bible can substantiate.

The Bible also contains may prophecies that came to exact fulfillment regarding empires that would come and go. Daniel 2 and Daniel 7 provide detailed prophecies regarding three kingdoms that would follow Babylon, the kingdom that existed during Daniel's time. Medo-Persia, Greece, and Rome rose exactly as prophesied. Daniel 11 provides a detailed list of individuals that Daniel prophesied would have major political roles during Old Testament times. The list is extremely detailed, and came to fulfillment exactly as stated. The three chapters mentioned are just the start of what God prophetically stated in the Scriptures. Once again, for complete documentation, Dr. John Walvoord's excellent scholarly book, *Every Prophecy of the Bible,* goes through each book in the Bible, documenting each prophecy and when God fulfilled the prophecy. This is evidence that demands your attention as you deliberate on the question, are you going to "a better place"?

The 500 prophecies that God has yet to fulfill all deal with what Christian theologians call end times events, defined as the specific things that God will bring to fulfillment exactly as stated. Those specific prophecies are beyond the scope of this book. Many excellent commentators on the Bible provide detailed lists of prophesied future events, and exactly how God's prophetic calendar will be fulfilled exactly as written. My personal favorite is Dr. Mark Hitchcock's detailed, scholarly, yet very readable work called *The End.*[7] The theological name for the study of God's prophesied yet future events as documented in the Scriptures is eschatology. God provides hundreds of details regarding such topics as the nation of Israel reforming after the Romans destroyed Israel in A.D. 70. The prophet Ezekiel prophesied in 590 B.C. that the dispersed Jewish people would one day return to the promised land (Ezekiel 37). Israel became a nation once again on May 14, 1948, and now God has miraculously drawn some seven million Jews from all around the world to go and live in Israel. God is the source of this miraculous migration of the Jewish people.

The Old and New Testament cite yet future wars with the exact countries named. Ezekiel 38-39 provides detailed prophesies regarding the specific countries that will invade Israel. The current Middle-East situation is setting the stage for the fulfillment of Bible prophecies. One would be foolish to reject Biblical prophecies in light of the hundreds that have already been literally fulfilled.

ALIGNMENT OF ANTI-ISRAELI NATIONS	
EZEKIEL 38-39	
GOG - LEADER	*PERSIA* – Includes Modern Day:
ROSH - *CHIEF*	▪ Afghanistan
MAGOG - RUSSIA	▪ Pakistan
TURKEY:	▪ Iran
▪ Meshech	*ETHIOPIA* Includes Modern Day:
▪ Tubal	▪ Somalia
▪ Gomer	▪ Sudan
▪ Togarmah	▪ Ethiopia
LIBYA	

---

[7] Mark Hitchcock, *The End* (Carol Stream, ILL.: Tyndale House Publishers, Inc.) 2012.

Eternity, heaven, hell, the lake of fire, and many other important subjects are all prophetic topics. This should be very encouraging as God has a perfect, proven record of fulfilling the first 500 prophecies in the Bible in chronological order. Therefore, when examining the Biblical evidence regarding one's eternal destiny in chapter one of this book, the reader should have confidence in the documented evidence.

Past, present, and future prophesied events provide a thrilling study, and provide undeniable documentation that the word of God is infallible (2 Timothy 3:16). The Bible claims that it not only contains the truth, but that its entire content is absolute truth.

> The entirety of Your word is truth, And every one of Your righteous judgments endures forever. (Psalm 119:160)

> And now, O Lord GOD, You are God, and Your words are true, and You have promised this goodness to Your servant. (2 Samuel 7:28)

> Sanctify them by Your truth. Your word is truth. (John 17:17)

> Pilate therefore said to Him, "Are You a king then?" Jesus answered, "You say rightly that I am a king. For this cause I was born, and for this cause I have come into the world, that I should bear witness to the truth. Everyone who is of the truth hears My voice." (John 18:37)

> Then he said to me, "These words are faithful and true." And the Lord God of the holy prophets sent His angel to show His servants the things which must shortly take place. (Revelation 22:6)

All the documentation presented thus far regarding the absolute truth of God's Word draws us to one of the most important verses that affects every person, past, present, and future. Please carefully read the following verse. "Jesus said to him, 'I am the way, the truth, and the life. No one comes to the Father except through Me.'"

(John 14:6) Jesus makes a very specific, exclusive statement. The Bible is straight forward, and leaves nothing to the imagination regarding the only judicially approved way for one to go to heaven.

This truth becomes a source of contention to those who believe there are, or should be, multiple avenues to heaven. Once again, the issue specifically regards where is the documented evidence to prove beyond a reasonable doubt that you are going to "a better place" when you die? Hope is not a plan. Belief in an unsubstantiated, undocumented, generational, or personal concept does not make it true. The Scriptures provide hundreds of documented, verifiable facts that no other belief system in the world can remotely come close to matching.

Therefore, when Jesus stated, "I am the way, the truth, and the life. No one comes to the Father except through Me" (John 14:6), He was not pulling a power play. He was lovingly attempting to tell the listeners that He was the plan, the absolute truth, the only way to true eternal life, as He was God incarnate, the One who left heaven to come to this sin cursed earth to provide the one and only way one may have eternal life. He came to provide you with eternal life through His death, burial, and resurrection. Luke records the very mission, the focal point, the reason for His coming to earth in Luke 19:10, "for the Son of Man has come to seek and to save that which was lost." The apostle Paul reiterates what Jesus told Luke, "This is a faithful saying and worthy of all acceptance, that Christ Jesus came into the world to save sinners." (1 Timothy 1:15) Jesus' mission could not be any clearer. Why did He go through with the mission?

> In this the love of God was manifested toward us, that God has sent His only begotten Son into the world, that we might live through Him. In this is love, not that we loved God, but that He loved us and sent His Son to be the propitiation *(atoning sacrifice)* for our sins. (1 John 4:9–10)

The contemporary governmental system often refers to information determined to contain verifiable facts, as "evidence based." There is debate among leadership regarding what constitutes a determination that is "evidence based." For those who embrace the concept of evidence-based information and outcomes, we will borrow that concept as we examine the Biblical evidence regarding, are you going to "a better place"?

The prophetic evidence presented to this point, and the inerrant claims of the Scripture are evidence based. The 500 prophecies that God fulfilled exactly as written are beyond the probability of human ability. The Scriptures prove themselves true, with verifiable, documented evidence. The prophetic Scriptures contain detailed and exact information that result in fulfillments that are precise, and match perfectly the original prophecy.

Are you going to "a better place"? The reader rightly desires to know if what has so far been presented, and if the remainder of this book, truly has evidence based, judicially approved, documented truth. If you were in a court of law, and you stood before the judge presenting 500 literal prophecies that have come to fruition with the exact details as stated in the original prophecy, without one point missed, would you as a judge take the presentation seriously? Again, the point of providing this information is not to trick the reader. It is not to make one believe something because the author stated it.

Please allow this simple explanation regarding the reason for this book. This project came to fruition for one reason. The Bible states that true Christians are known by their love for others (John 13:35). The intent is to provide you, the reader with the only assurance of eternal life provided through documented, verifiable evidence found in the Word of God. Every piece of evidence presented is based solely upon the verifiable truths found in the Scriptures. Referring to the Bible as the Word of God is not presumptuous, for the verifiable evidence is overwhelming, and documented.

Before moving to more documented evidence, where do you stand on your understanding of, are you going to "a better place"? Have you accepted the free gift of eternal life by acknowledging you are a sinner (Romans 3:23)? Have you acknowledged that you are deserving of eternal separation from God in eternal torment based on the penalty for sin (Romans 6:23, Revelation 21:8)? Do you believe that Jesus Christ is God's Son, that He left the Father's presence, came to this earth as a virgin born baby, and willingly went to the cross, died, was buried, and three days later rose from the dead as the payment for your sin debt (John 3:16; 1 Corinthians 15:1-4)? Finally, have you not only acknowledged these facts, but have you placed your faith alone in the promise of Ephesians 2:8-9, "For by grace you have been saved through faith, and that not of yourselves; it is the gift of God, not of works, lest anyone should boast"? If you have, that is wonderful. If not, consider accepting that free gift right now before moving to the next chapter. If you are ready to accept the gift of salvation, maybe you would like to tell God right now that you are accepting Jesus Christ as your Savior. Here is simply a suggested prayer to let the Lord know what you are doing in your heart:

> Dear God, I know I have sinned and do not deserve to go to heaven. However, this very moment, I believe that Jesus Christ is God, that He came down from heaven in human form, was crucified, died, was buried, and rose from the dead three days later to pay for my sins. I now receive the free gift of eternal life by placing my faith in what Jesus did for me, by sacrificing His own life on the cross. I realize I cannot earn heaven by my good works, but only by accepting what the Lord Jesus Christ did for me. Thank you for saving me from the penalty of sin and promising to take me to heaven when I die. In Jesus' name, Amen.

I would encourage you to contact me and share your decision to place your faith in Jesus Christ, or if you still have questions, I will be happy to answer them. You can email me at
Rich@ProphecyFocusMinistries.com
or call me at (414) 788-6010.

Are You Going to a Better Place?

Are You Going to a Better Place?

Are You Going to a Better Place?

Are You Going to a Better Place?

Are You Going to a Better Place?

Are You Going to a Better Place?

Are You Going to a Better Place?

Are You Going to a Better Place?

Are You Going to a Better Place?

Are You Going to a Better Place?

Are You Going to a Better Place?

Are You Going to a Better Place?

Are You Going to a Better Place?

Are You Going to a Better Place?

Are You Going to a Better Place?

Are You Going to a Better Place?

Are You Going to a Better Place?

Are You Going to a Better Place?

CHAPTER 3
Evidence Bearing 100% Accuracy - You Will Die

We will examine one absolutely, undeniable fact. No person in the history of the known world escapes death, barring two specific people discussed in the Old Testament, Enoch (Genesis 5:24) and Elijah (2 Kings 2:11), who were both taken to heaven without dying. Death is an undeniable fact, which forces people to contemplate their eternal destiny.

The reasonable question is, why do people die? The simple, but only partially true answer is that all will die because they eventually get sick, the body wears out, or some unfortunate, horrendous tragedy takes place, which takes someone's life. Regardless of how death comes, there is a certainty that everyone will experience death.

The Bible reveals the cause of all sickness and death, which was the original sin of Adam, which this book summarized in chapter one. Examining how sin and death entered the world provides additional evidence in the quest for undeniable truth.

Exodus 20:11 reveals that God created everything in the universe, including angels. The Scriptures reveal that the most beautiful and perfect angel that God created He named Lucifer (also called Satan).

'Thus says the Lord GOD: "You were the seal of perfection, Full of wisdom and perfect in beauty. You were in Eden, the garden of God; Every precious stone was your covering: The sardius, topaz, and diamond, Beryl, onyx, and jasper, Sapphire, turquoise, and emerald with gold. The workmanship of your timbrels and pipes Was prepared for you on the day you were created." You were the anointed cherub who covers; I established you; You were on the holy mountain of God; You walked back and forth in the midst of fiery stones. You were perfect in your ways from the day you were created, Till iniquity was found in you. "By the abundance of your trading you became filled with violence within, and you sinned; Therefore I cast you as a profane thing out of the mountain of God; And I destroyed you, O covering cherub, from the midst of the fiery stones. "Your heart was lifted up because of your beauty; You corrupted your wisdom for the sake of your splendor; I cast you to the ground, I laid you before kings, that they might gaze at you. (Ezekiel 28:12–17)

The Scriptures provide additional evidence regarding the rebellion of Satan against God.

"How you are fallen from heaven, O Lucifer, son of the morning! How you are cut down to the ground, you who weakened the nations! For you have said in your heart:
'**I will** ascend into heaven,
I will exalt my throne above the stars of God;
I will also sit on the mount of the congregation On the farthest sides of the north;
I will ascend above the heights of the clouds,
I will be like the Most High.'
Yet you shall be brought down to Sheol, to the lowest depths of the Pit. (Isaiah 14:12–15)

The five *I wills* of Satan reveal that this created, once-perfect angel rebelled against God Himself, and ever since that time has sought to destroy what God created, which includes every single person who ever lived. What caused Lucifer, now known as Satan, to rebel so violently against God and His creation? God tucked away the answers in the book of Job. God created the angels before He created anything else. The angels, referred to several times in the Bible as the sons of God, watched as God created everything in the universe (Job 38:4-7). God described Lucifer as a beautiful, perfect angel (Ezekiel 28:12). However, something radically changed in the mind of Lucifer. After creating the angelic realm, God created Adam and Eve. God gave them a specific charge that would turn Lucifer's world upside down.

Then God said, "Let Us make man in Our image, according to Our likeness; *let them have dominion* over the fish of the sea, over the birds of the air, and over the cattle, over all the earth and over every creeping thing that creeps on the earth." So God created man in His own image; in the image of God He created him; male and female He created them. Then God blessed them, and God said to them, "Be fruitful and multiply; fill the earth and subdue it; *have dominion* over the fish of the sea, over the birds of the air, and over every living thing that moves on the earth." (Genesis 1:26-28)

Lucifer was the model of perfection, and before God created Adam and Eve on the final day of creation, Lucifer, for all intents and purposes, had dominion over everything that God made in the first five days of creation. Now Lucifer finds out that God Himself granted Adam and Eve dominion over all of creation. Lucifer, who obviously had a free will, exercised his will to rebel against God's determination that someone else would have dominion. Thus, the description God provided in Ezekiel 28 and Isaiah 14 regarding Lucifer's rebellion now makes perfect sense.

Lucifer began his quest to destroy God's perfectly created universe. He targeted Eve and, as already cited, his temptation of Eve resulted in her temptation of Adam, and the subsequent fall of humanity from perfection to corruption, further resulting in the sin nature, and guaranteed death. "Therefore, just as through one man [Adam] sin entered the world, and death through sin, and thus death spread to all men, because all sinned" (Romans 5:12). The documentation just cited verifies exactly why everyone will experience death, and enter their eternal destiny of heaven or hell. This is an undeniable fact based on evidence from the Scriptures.

Theologians refer to Genesis 3:15 as the *protoevangelium*, or the first giving of the gospel.[8] "And I will put enmity Between you and the woman, And between your seed and her Seed; He shall bruise your head, And you shall bruise His heel." (Genesis 3:15) Immediately after the fall of humanity, God provided the path for removal of the penalty of spiritual death (Hebrews 9:27; Revelation 21:8). Let us examine Genesis 3:15 in an expanded form:

---

[8]John D. Barry et al., eds., "Protevangelium," *The Lexham Bible Dictionary* (Bellingham, WA: Lexham Press, 2016).

And I [God] will put enmity between you [Satan] and the woman [Eve's descendants], And between your seed [Satan's demonic realm] and her Seed [The seed of Mary, Jesus Christ]; He [Jesus Christ] shall bruise your (Satan's] head, And you [Satan] shall bruise His [Jesus Christ's] heel.

The Scriptures from this point forward, begin to unfold God's plan to save people from the horrific consequences of sin. God's plan of salvation, also known as His redemptive plan, as first revealed in Genesis 3:15, is further defined in the following summary excerpted from *The Lexham Bible Dictionary*:

God spoke to the serpent (vv. 14–15), to Eve (v. 16), and to Adam (vv. 17–19). God's words to the serpent included (a) the announcement that the snake, crawling and eating dust, would be a perpetual reminder to mankind of temptation and the Fall, and (b) an oracle about the power behind the snake. God said there would be a perpetual struggle between satanic forces and mankind. It would be between Satan and the woman, and their respective offspring or "seeds." The "offspring" of the woman was Cain, then all humanity at large, and then Christ and those collectively in Him. The "offspring" of the serpent includes demons and anyone serving his kingdom of darkness, those whose "father" is the devil (John 8:44). Satan would cripple mankind (you will strike at his heel), but *the* Seed, Christ, would deliver the fatal blow (He will crush your head).[9]

God made you for fellowship, and He desires to spend eternity with You. But the choice is yours. Yes, you are a victim of Adam's original sin. Adam's transgression resulted in the sin nature being passed to every person through the seed of their father. (Romans 5:12) The Scriptures reveal the catastrophic results that you not only possess the sin nature, but you literally perform sinful acts, as all have sinned. (Romans 3:23) But God has allowed you to be the jury, and the judge on your eternal fate. Are you going to "a better place"?

---

[9]Allen P. Ross, "Genesis," in *The Bible Knowledge Commentary: An Exposition of the Scriptures*, ed. J. F. Walvoord and R. B. Zuck, vol. 1 (Wheaton, IL: Victor Books, 1985), 33.

God cursed multiple things as recorded in Genesis chapter three, as the direct result of Satan's rebellion against God.

So the LORD God said to the serpent: "Because you have done this, You are cursed more than all cattle, And more than every beast of the field; On your belly you shall go, And you shall eat dust All the days of your life.

And I will put enmity between you and the woman, and between your seed and her Seed; He shall bruise your head, And you shall bruise His heel."

To the woman He said: "I will greatly multiply your sorrow and your conception; In pain you shall bring forth children; Your desire shall be for your husband, and he shall rule over you."

Then to Adam He said, "Because you have heeded the voice of your wife, and have eaten from the tree of which I commanded you, saying, 'You shall not eat of it': "Cursed is the ground for your sake; In toil you shall eat of it all the days of your life. Both thorns and thistles it shall bring forth for you, and you shall eat the herb of the field. In the sweat of your face you shall eat bread till you return to the ground, For out of it you were taken; For dust you are, and to dust you shall return [death begins]." (Genesis 3:14–19)

Death is a hard reality for many people to comprehend and accept, and while people deal with this reality in different ways, no one can escape it. Once again, this question is front and center: are you going to "a better place," or "a dreadful place" for all eternity?

My first encounter with the harshness and permanence of death occurred when I was nine years old. I had a wonderful relationship with my grandparents. They enjoyed having me and my sisters to their home, and of course they spoiled us, which certainly every child enjoys. I had a very close relationship with my mother's dad. Grandpa always gave me the best presents, and we had a great time hanging out together. I spent many nights over at my grandparents' home in Illinois. Those were very special days, and ones that I cherished.

My mother received a phone call at our home that I will never forget. Her mother was on the phone, and I could tell that something was dreadfully wrong. My mom and dad gathered the family together and told us we needed to immediately go to grandpa and grandma's home, which was about 30 minutes away. My mom informed us during the car ride that grandpa had died. The concept of death was sobering, but at that time I did not fully grasp what it meant.

We arrived at my grandparent's home, and I sat in the living room quietly observing my mom, dad, and grandmother. I found out that grandpa was lying on the floor in the bathroom, and the adults would not allow me to go down the hall and see him. After some time passed, two men entered the home with a gurney. They went down the hall, and after several minutes, the men were pushing the gurney with a black bag on top, containing the lifeless body of my beloved grandpa. Though I knew cognitively what had transpired, the reality of death still did not have any emotional impact on me.

Several days later, my mother had me put on my suit, and get ready to go to grandpa's funeral. My grandparents did not attend church, and therefore, the funeral service took place in a cold, dark mausoleum.

When we arrived, I looked in the open casket and saw the still body of my beloved grandpa. After a few moments, the casket closed, never to be opened again. The service ended and my family went back to the car. I sat in the back seat, and without warning, my heart broke and the tears flowed in heart wrenching agony. The reality that grandpa was dead, and that I would never see him again, hit me very hard. Heaven and hell meant nothing to me at the time, and all I could process was the fact that my dear grandpa was gone forever. My sorrow and grief were overwhelming at the time. The reality of the finality of death shook my young mind. From that time forward, my search for what takes place after death became much more important to me.

Maybe you have experienced the loss of a loved one and attended their funeral. As an ordained pastor, I have conducted and attended many funerals. I have observed the many varied emotional responses family members and friends display at funerals.

The family and friends of the person who passed away enter the room, where in most cases the person is lying in a casket, to see the person one last time. Some visitors show little or no emotion. Others, suffering a significant loss, cry softly, and still others wail uncontrollably. Some literally fall across the casket overcome with grief at the loss of their loved one. The fact that most people have no assurance that they will ever see their loved one again is deeply troubling to me. Regardless of how one responds to someone's death, if they have no assurance that their loved one is in "a better place," that is a very disturbing scenario.

It is a horrible experience to watch people who have no hope (no assurance of eternity in heaven) journey through the grieving process. Some people believe there's nothing beyond this life. The last breath results in the body going in the ground or urn, never to experience life again. For others, death is, or hoped to be, the beginning of peace and rest in "a better place". What is the truth? What really takes place at death? What does the verifiable evidence prove? Where will those who die spend eternity? A dead person has no ability to change their eternal situation. The gavel drops at death, and the verdict stands on the person's eternal destiny.

Now is the appropriate time to once again reiterate the fact that the person who died was their own jury and judge regarding their response to the Bible's documented evidence. Those who accepted the documented, verifiable evidence of the world's best-selling book, the Bible, on God's precise way to go to Heaven, will enjoy eternity with their Savior, the Lord Jesus Christ. Those who determined that God's way was not their way, unfortunately will suffer the consequences for eternity. The very reason this book exists is to beg you to consider the evidence, and make the only decision that makes sense.

Your decision is a judicially binding verdict in God's court, where He will sentence you to the eternally binding choice you make. Those who accept God's free gift of salvation by placing their faith alone in what Jesus accomplished for them in His death, burial, and resurrection, receive eternal life with the Lord Jesus in heaven (Ephesians 2:8-9). Those who attempt to get to heaven another way will incur the

31

righteous judgment of God, receive the just sentence of eternal separation from Him, and be cast into the lake of fire (Revelation 21:8).

This book began with the statement that you are a victim of the original sin of Adam (Romans 5:12). Based on Adam's sin, you inherited the sin nature, and are now the defendant who must determine your eternal destiny based on documented evidence. You are the jury and the judge of what will happen to you after you take your last breath. Immediately your eternal destiny, based upon the verifiable evidence provided, becomes your reality. What you determine to do prior to death with the Scriptural documentation will guarantee your eternal fate.

Like a person in a home on fire, you can choose to stay in the building and suffer the horrible consequences, or you can quickly remove yourself from an excruciating death. You still have time to react to the evidence provided. However, your time on earth could be short. You have no guarantee of taking one more breath. Once again, the question is before you. If you have not already done so, are you now ready to accept the gift of eternal life in heaven, made completely possible by accepting the Lord Jesus Christ's death, burial, and resurrection as complete payment for your sin? Are you guaranteed that you will go to "a better place"?

CHAPTER 4
Evidence Your Good Works Are Not Admissible
Faith in Christ vs. Works Based Religions

We now come to the most difficult topic of this book, which is, can good works guarantee a person a place in heaven? The world's religions all unequivocally place a strong emphasis on one's personal lifestyle and good works to take them to "a better place." Many religions require self-deprivation or an ascetic lifestyle to gain favor with God. What should you as an individual trust in for your eternal destiny? This is the question that must remain in critical focus.

There are individuals who scoff at the idea of doing good works; they could care less whether they spend eternity in heaven or hell, based upon their understanding of the two alternatives. Their concept of hell is far from a Biblical definition. They see hell as a fun place where they will spend eternity with their friends, drinking, partying, and having a great time. This may seem like a bizarre scenario to you, but I guarantee you that I have heard a significant number of people state those exact words.

Certain religious groups teach that one can obtain deliverance from a temporary place called purgatory or even hell itself by performing good works during their life. Certain religious groups teach that after one dies, they can still do good works, or suffer temporarily, and work their way out of purgatory or hell itself. This false teaching is clearly incompatible with the Scriptures:

> He [Jesus Christ] then would have had to suffer often since the foundation of the world; but now, once at the end of the ages, He has appeared to put away sin by the sacrifice of Himself. And as it is appointed for men to die once, but after this the judgment, so Christ was offered once to bear the sins of many. To those who eagerly wait for Him He will appear a second time, apart from sin, for salvation. (Hebrews 9:26–28)

Many strongly believe that if their good works outweigh their inappropriate and sinful conduct that they will one day enjoy the beauty of heaven with God. Every major religion teaches as *gospel truth* that works are the only way to enter heaven's glory and spend eternity with God. Many who call themselves Christians strongly embrace the concept that *good works* or their good lifestyle will get them to heaven. There are denominations that teach that baptism or the Eucharist, also referred to by certain Christian groups as Communion or the Lord's table, will guarantee them eternal life in heaven. Others believe that going through catechism guarantees them a place in heaven. What does the documented evidence (the Bible) state?

> For by grace [God's free unmerited gift] you have been saved through faith, and that not of yourselves; it is the gift of God, not of works, lest anyone should boast. (Ephesians 2:8–9)

> For God so loved the world that He gave His only begotten Son, that whoever believes in Him should not perish but have everlasting life. For God did not send His Son into the world to condemn the world, but that the world through Him might be saved. He who believes in Him is not condemned; but he who does not believe is condemned already, because he has not believed in the name of the only begotten Son of God. (John 3:16–18)

The Scriptures provide a very detailed account of what *good works* can accomplish. I have quoted Ephesians 2:8-9 several times. The very next verse, Ephesians 2:10, provides the chronological point at which *good works* actually come into play with God.

> For by grace you have been saved through faith, and that not of yourselves; it is the gift of God, not of works, lest anyone should boast. For we are His workmanship, created in Christ Jesus for good works, which God prepared beforehand that we should walk in them. (Ephesians 2:8–10)

Ephesians 2:8-10 provides the chronological answer to the value of good works. Verse 8 identifies the subject, *you*, referring to those who have been saved by placing their faith in the free gift of eternal life through what Christ accomplished in His death, burial, and resurrection.

"For by grace *you* have been saved through faith, and that not of yourselves; it is the gift of God, not of works, lest anyone should boast." The Scripture provides in verse 10 the next thing that a person who *is saved*, or has received the gift of eternal life, is expected to do with their life. Verse 10 states, "For *we* are His workmanship, created in Christ Jesus for good works, which God prepared beforehand that we should walk in them." The Biblical chronology of a person's life should be as follows.

Sinner ➡ Hears Gospel ➡ Comes to Saving Faith in Jesus ➡ Performs Good Works Out of Gratitude and Devotion to the Savior (not to earn salvation)

"Religion" or humankind's normal response or comprehension regarding the concept of what good works accomplish is the following.

Sinner ➡ Performs Good Works ➡ Hopes to Get to Heaven

"Hope" is not a plan, and neither is it God's gospel. God gives a very detailed account of what one's alleged good works accomplish before placing their faith alone in Jesus Christ and what He alone accomplished on the cross.

> What then? Are we better than they? Not at all. For we have previously charged both Jews and Greeks that they are all under sin. As it is written: *"There is none righteous, no, not one; There is none who understands; There is none who seeks after God. They have all turned aside; They have together become unprofitable; There is none who does good, no, not one."* "Their throat is an open tomb; With their tongues they have practiced deceit"; "The poison of asps is under their lips"; "Whose mouth is full of cursing and bitterness." "Their feet are swift to shed blood; Destruction and misery are in their ways; And the way of peace they have not known." "There is no fear of God before their eyes." (Romans 3:9–18)

The prophet Isaiah clearly stated,

> But we are all like an unclean thing, and all our righteousnesses are like filthy rags. (Isaiah 64:6)

God leaves nothing to speculation, and His judicial decision is that humankind is incapable of performing anything considered good before they receive the free gift of eternal life by placing their faith in what Jesus alone accomplished on the cross.

Romans 3 continues to explicitly declare God's absolute position on the issue of good works versus faith alone in Christ regarding the question of, are you going to "a better place"?

> Now we know that whatever the law says, it says to those who are under the law, that every mouth may be stopped, and all the world may become guilty before God. Therefore by the deeds of the law no flesh will be justified in His sight, for by the law is the knowledge of sin.

> But now the righteousness of God apart from the law is revealed, being witnessed by the Law and the Prophets, even the righteousness of God, through faith in Jesus Christ, to all and on all who believe. For there is no difference; for *all have sinned and fall short of the glory of God, being justified freely by His grace through the redemption that is in Christ Jesus.* (Romans 3:19-26)

Where do good works fall into God's plan for salvation? Nowhere. The Bible clearly states that no person can earn their salvation (a place in heaven) by performing good works. Instead, one must accept the free gift of eternal life by faith. Good works occur subsequent to salvation, defined as the point in time when one accepts the grace of God, and places their faith in the finished work of Jesus Christ that He alone accomplished through His death, burial, and resurrection (1 Corinthians 15:1-4).

Every person who attempts to earn their salvation by producing good works are in the proverbial sense spinning their wheels in the mud. God does not grant any favor or merit for a person's attempt at pleasing Him before they humbly accept His Son, and the sacrifice He went through to completely pay their sin debt.

Do *good works* matter to God? The simple answer is good works absolutely matter to God after one places their faith in His Son for forgiveness of sin, and they receive the promise of eternal life. Good works are an outward expression of the gratitude that one has for God, after receiving the free gift of eternal life, not before. Unfortunately, there are many people who completely misunderstand this critical piece of evidence. Religious leaders across the world indoctrinate their followers with a false narrative, and false gospel, of a works-based religion that will allegedly take them to *a better place.*

What evidence do these religious leaders provide? Where is the documentation? Do they possess verifiable evidence to substantiate their claims? Do they produce a document that contains 500 specific prophecies written a short time to hundreds of years before they came to exact fulfillment? Do those who state they substantiate their claims with the Bible produce the passages to back up their position?

Your eternal destiny is dependent on getting God's plan for eternal life correct, guaranteeing that you are definitely going to *a better place.* Regardless of your church affiliation or lack thereof, your particular choice of religion, or your potential disdain for religion, it does not change the documented, verifiable facts presented in the one book that provides clear, convincing evidence that you can only go to *a better place* by accepting God's gift as provided exclusively through the death, burial, and resurrection of Jesus Christ.

The apostle John provides the answer to one of His disciples who had questions regarding the path to heaven. Jesus answered the question in the following passage.

> "Let not your heart be troubled; you believe in God, believe also in Me. In My Father's house are many mansions; if it were not so, I would have told you. I go to prepare a place for you. And if I go and prepare a place for you, I will come again and receive you to Myself; that where I am, there you may be also. And where I go you know, and the way you know."
>
> Thomas said to Him, "Lord, we do not know where You are going, and how can we know the way?" *Jesus said to him, "I am the way, the truth, and the life. No one comes to the Father except through Me.* (John 14:1–6)

Jesus left nothing to the imagination or speculation. He stated who He was, His relationship to God the Father, and the pathway to heaven, which was only through Him. Jesus Himself said nothing to Thomas about producing good works, as good works are evidence of faith in Jesus Christ, not a precursor.

Galatians chapter one provides a strong admonition to those who teach a false gospel. The apostle Paul wrote the book of Galatians under the inspiration of the Holy Spirit, the third member of the Trinity. Paul states two times the penalty for any religious leader who teaches a false gospel.

> I marvel that you are turning away so soon from Him who called you in the grace of Christ, to a different gospel, which is not another; but there are some who trouble you and want to pervert the gospel of Christ. But even if we, or an angel from heaven, preach any other gospel to you than what we have preached to you, let him be accursed. As we have said before, so now I say again, if anyone preaches any other gospel to you than what you have received, let him be accursed. (Galatians 1:6–9)

The gravity of what the apostle Paul reveals in the passage cannot be overstated. Paul is literally stating that anyone who tells another person a false gospel is deserving of eternal punishment. Why? Once again, the Scriptures give the answer. "My brethren, let not many of you become teachers, knowing that we shall receive a stricter judgment." (James 3:1) God holds religious leaders accountable for their teachings. Those who lead people down the path of a false gospel, endangering the listener from receiving the true gospel are accursed. Genesis 3:15 vividly states that God judged Satan for misleading Eve and Adam. Satan's eternal penalty for misleading not only Adam and Eve, but thousands of people around the world over thousands of years is the eternal lake of fire. Satan, also known as the devil, and serpent of old (Revelation 12:9; 20:2), faces the irrevocable penalty of the eternal lake of fire, at the end of the age.

> The devil [Satan], who deceived them, was cast into the lake of fire and brimstone where the beast and the false prophet are. And they will be tormented day and night forever and ever.

(Revelation 20:10)

God holds people accountable for their *bad works* when they fail to place their faith in the finished work of Jesus Christ. As already shown from the evidence, good works have no value in providing a pathway to *a better place*. God only entertains the concept of good works after a person accepts the gospel of the marvelous grace of God (John 3:16-17; Galatians 3:11–14; Ephesians 2:8-9; Titus 3:5-6).

Theologians and Bible scholars apply a very specific set of interpretive rules, called hermeneutics, when reading and studying the Scriptures. One could compare the discipline of hermeneutics to what the Supreme Court employs when they examine issues in the Constitution that require further definition or interpretation. The authors of the Constitution knew exactly what they meant when they wrote the document. However, when others through the centuries read the Constitution, their presuppositions, cultural bias, alternative worldview, or other potential input may generate a conclusion that conflicts with previous interpretations of the Constitution. When disagreements of interpretation occur, those who spent a lifetime in the legal profession use their knowledge and experience to provide the legal community with their interpretation and final decision on the rule of law. Their decisions impact what takes place on this earth in the judicial setting.

When God wrote the Scriptures, there were no errors, no contradictions, and He knew exactly what He meant. The following passages attest to the inerrancy and sufficiency of Scripture.

> Scripture is given by inspiration of God [God breathed], and is profitable for doctrine, for reproof, for correction, for instruction in righteousness, that the man of God may be complete, thoroughly equipped for every good work. (2 Timothy 3:16–17)

> The grass withers, the flower fades, But the word of our God stands forever." (Isaiah 40:8)

> The counsel of the LORD stands forever, The plans of His heart to all generations. (Psalm 33:11)

Jesus Christ is the same yesterday, today, and forever. (Hebrews 13:8)

For I testify to everyone who hears the words of the prophecy of this book: If anyone adds to these things, God will add to him the plagues that are written in this book; and if anyone takes away from the words of the book of this prophecy, God shall take away his part from the Book of Life, from the holy city, and from the things which are written in this book. (Revelation 22:18–19)

Bible scholars who embrace the inerrancy and infallibility of Scripture hold to four key elements of Bible interpretation. The elements include interpreting the Bible according to its historical, contextual, grammatical, and literal meaning.[10] Bible scholars and readers should always strive to understand the Scriptures exactly as God intended, without man's divergent thoughts skewing the meaning of the Biblical text. Will God take you to heaven based on your good works? The Scriptures, God's final word, provide the answer. Understanding the importance of properly interpreting the Scriptures provide the introduction to one of the most misunderstood subjects in the Bible, baptism.

Theologians, pastors, and priests have significant divergent conclusions on the efficacy of baptism. Does baptism provide a guaranteed avenue to heaven? Parents take their babies to church to be baptized, trusting that their child will be taken to heaven should the unthinkable take place. The issue morphs into the conclusion that baptism provides a guaranteed place in heaven through adulthood, regardless of whether the person ever accepted the gift of eternal life through placing their faith in the death, burial, and resurrection of Christ.

Concluding that baptism has the permanent ability to save

---

[10] Roy B. Zuck, *Basic Bible Interpretation* (Colorado Springs, CO.: David C. Cook, 1991), 241-244.

someone from their sins makes baptism a work, and works do not take anyone to heaven. (Ephesians 2:8-9; Titus 3:5-6) Scripture points out that Christian baptism always follows belief in Jesus Christ. Scripture, furthermore, never records Jesus, the disciples, apostles, or anyone else baptizing one single baby. Right now, you may be in a serious conundrum, as your religious leader told you something antithetical to the statements just made. If you are not a student of the Bible, a simple internet search on the subject, querying the Bible for infant baptism will provide you the facts. Catechisms, liturgy, manmade statements, and conclusions are not the Bible, the only authoritative words of God Himself. If you are counting on baptism to take you to heaven, may I encourage you to now look at the provided Biblical evidence.

John the Baptist baptized many people, as recorded in Matthew, Mark, Luke, and John. The people came, repented of their sins, and then John baptized them. Matthew records this exact chronological sequence.

> Now John himself was clothed in camel's hair, with a leather belt around his waist; and his food was locusts and wild honey. Then Jerusalem, all Judea, and all the region around the Jordan went out to him and were baptized by him in the Jordan, confessing their sins. (Matthew 3:4–6)

Scripture is clear that those John baptized confessed their sins, something impossible for a baby to accomplish.

John condemned those who observed him baptize and were critical of his actions. "But when he [John] saw many of the Pharisees and Sadducees coming to his baptism, he said to them, 'Brood of vipers! Who warned you to flee from the wrath to come?'" (Matthew 3:7) John's baptism was for repentance in preparation for the revealing of the Lord Jesus Christ. Those who questioned the authority of John and the message he conveyed doubted the prophetic Scriptures.

John also clearly knew that Jesus, his contemporary, would provide salvation through what He would accomplish in His death, burial, and resurrection.

> I [John] indeed baptize you with water unto repentance, but He [Jesus] who is coming after me is mightier than I, whose sandals I am not worthy to carry. He will baptize you with the Holy Spirit

and fire. His winnowing fan is in His hand, and He will thoroughly clean out His threshing floor, and gather His wheat into the barn; but He will burn up the chaff with unquenchable fire." (Matthew 3:11–12)

Subsequent to the death, burial, resurrection, and ascension of Jesus Christ, the book of Acts records numerous baptisms performed. Every baptism recorded includes only those who exercised their free will to first believe on the Lord Jesus Christ, and then they were baptized as a sign of their faith in Jesus Christ. (Acts 2, 8, 9, 10, 16, 18, 19, 22)

The evidence provides a very clear and convincing argument that Scriptural Christian baptism always occurs after a person realizes they are a sinner, and subsequently placed their faith in what Jesus accomplished for them in His death, burial, and resurrection. The Biblical argument is overwhelming that baptism is always subsequent to a person understanding their sinful state, and in desperate need of the Savior, before baptism. Therefore, the Scriptural truth remains intact that one is saved strictly by grace through faith (Ephesians 2:8-9), and that Christian baptism is only an outward expression by a believer in Jesus Christ, of their faith, which they placed in His completed work on the cross through His death, burial, and resurrection.

God looks forward to every person performing good works for Him in the proper Biblical chronological order. God's order comprises to first humble oneself and admit they are a sinner (Romans 3:23); second, understand the penalty for sin is the eternal lake of fire (Revelation 21:8); third, realize that Jesus Christ, God's Son left heaven's glory, was crucified, buried, and three days later rose from the dead (1 Corinthians 15:3-4); fourth, by faith alone, receive the free gift of eternal life (Ephesians 2:8-9), and finally, perform good works out of love and a desire to serve their Savior, Jesus Christ (Ephesians 2:10).

CHAPTER 5
Evidence the "Supreme Court" Will Judge

The Scriptures leave nothing to chance when it comes to God's final meeting with every single person throughout history who refused to accept God's free gift of eternal life. The Bible provides the documentation in Revelation 20, which describes a very real encounter that each person who failed to come to faith in the Lord will have with Jesus Christ. The Scriptural evidence regarding God's final sentence of condemnation is very clear and concise, and yes, terrifying. Carefully consider the gravity of the following passage of Scripture.

> Then I saw a great white throne and Him who sat on it, from whose face the earth and the heaven fled away. And there was found no place for them. And I saw the dead, small and great, standing before God, and books were opened. And another book was opened, which is the Book of Life. And the dead were judged according to their works, by the things which were written in the books. The sea gave up the dead who were in it, and Death and Hades delivered up the dead who were in them. And they were judged, each one according to his works. Then Death and Hades were cast into the lake of fire. This is the second death. And anyone not found written in the Book of Life was cast into the lake of fire (Revelation 20:11-15).

The Supreme Court Judge, the Lord Jesus Christ, will open the books, and after presenting the documented evidence for each person's life, He will render the final sentence. At that point, God will hold each individual personally accountable for the decisions they made before taking their last breath. The Supreme Court simply verifies the decision made by each person, and then states and enforces their eternal sentence.

The Bible identifies a book called the *Book of Life*. Revelation 20 states that anyone whose name is not found in the *Book of Life* will be cast into the lake of fire. This truth is not popular and certainly not politically correct. However, despite one's potential rejection of the concept, it remains a Biblical, judicial determination that the Supreme

Court Judge, Jesus Christ, will enforce based upon His righteous judgment.

Each person whose name is written in God's *Book of Life* is guaranteed to spend eternity with God. The opposite is true for those whose names are not written in the *Book of Life*. They will enter the lake of fire with an imperishable body and suffer for all eternity apart from God. God documents these facts not for you to bristle at or deny, but for you to receive as a forewarning of the devastating consequences of not receiving the Lord Jesus Christ as your personal Savior. Jesus Christ, the Supreme Court Judge, provides the documentation ahead of time in the world's best-selling and most well-known book, the Bible, allowing all who will listen to His Word the opportunity to realize the significant and eternal cost of refusing to place one's faith in the Lord Jesus.

God states in 2 Peter 3:9 that He is not willing that one person should suffer an eternity apart from Him. God loves every single person, and therefore, He provided the information up front on how to avoid the penalty of sin. However, God gave every person a free will, and each person can choose to accept or reject His offer of eternal life. God never forces anyone to accept His love. God furthermore states that whosoever will may come to Him. (John 3:16; Romans 10:13)

The apostle Paul reveals in the book of Romans, that God uses everything He created as information pointing to the fact that God exists, and therefore, no one is excused from the necessity of seeking the truths about Him.

> For the wrath of God is revealed from heaven against all ungodliness and unrighteousness of men, who suppress the truth in unrighteousness, because what may be known of God is manifest in them, for God has shown it to them. For since the creation of the world His invisible attributes are clearly seen, being understood by the things that are made, even His eternal power and Godhead, so that they are without excuse.
> (Romans 1:18-20)

Now is the time for each individual to consider their eternal destiny. God never encourages selfish living, but when it comes to making the eternally binding decision of one's eternal destiny, each individual must decide for themselves. No one can make this eternal decision for you or for another person.

Revelation 20 states several times that God judges each person at the Great White Throne based on the content of the books. God does not describe what each book contains, yet, based on the context, the works each person performed while alive on the earth, are known and recorded. Each person will have the list of their works read to them, and then God will render His eternal sentence.

Imagine standing before the Lord Jesus, and having Him reveal every immoral, unethical, selfish, unkind, evil thought you ever had? Jesus Himself stated "For nothing is secret that will not be revealed, nor anything hidden that will not be known and come to light." (Luke 8:17) God warns every person exactly what will take place after death, and how to avoid condemnation and enjoy the glory of heaven in His presence.

The Scriptures reveal that those who receive eternal life through faith in Jesus Christ are *justified*.

> But when the kindness and the love of God our Savior toward man appeared, not by works of righteousness which we have done, but according to His mercy He saved us, through the washing of regeneration and renewing of the Holy Spirit, whom He poured out on us abundantly through Jesus Christ our Savior, that having been justified by His grace we should become heirs according to the hope of eternal life. (Titus 3:4-7)

> Knowing that a man is not justified by the works of the law but by faith in Jesus Christ, even we have believed in Christ Jesus, that we might be justified by faith in Christ and not by the works of the law; for by the works of the law no flesh shall be justified. (Galatians 2:16)

The word *justified* has a deep theological meaning that the following excerpt brings to light.

> **JUS'TIFY, JUSTIFICA'TION** These terms involve one of the fundamental principles of the Christian faith. They stand opposite to "condemn" and "condemnation." In their evangelical use they denote that act of God's sovereign grace by which he accepts and receives those who believe in Christ as just and righteous. Justification includes the pardon of sins and the imputation of the righteousness of Christ. The merits of Christ are the only ground of justification; faith is the only means of justification; good works are the necessary fruit or

evidence of justification. The Epistles of Paul to the Galatians and the Romans give the fullest exposition of this doctrine.[11]

Some astute defense lawyers may think they just discovered a loophole proving that works do have merit in gaining salvation. Revelation 20 clearly states that people will be judged by their works, but the context of the text defines the meaning. The Scriptures provide the absolute documented evidence in 2 Corinthians 5:8, and Revelation 19:6-9 and 20:4-6. Before the Great White Throne judgment occurs, God has already resurrected all *believers* in the Lord, and each is in the presence of Jesus Christ. The white throne judgment is the specific time, literally at the end of the world or age, when God sentences all *unbelievers*. Furthermore, a review of Romans 3 documents that no person can produce good works before placing their faith in Jesus Christ.

As it is written: "There is none righteous, no, not one; There is none who understands; There is none who seeks after God. They have all turned aside; They have together become unprofitable; There is none who does good, no, not one." "Their throat is an open tomb; With their tongues they have practiced deceit"; "The poison of asps is under their lips"; "Whose mouth is full of cursing and bitterness." "Their feet are swift to shed blood; Destruction and misery are in their ways; And the way of peace they have not known." "There is no fear of God before their eyes."
(Romans 3:10-18)

Ephesians 2:8-10 clarifies the chronological sequence of faith in Christ before a person can produce good works.

For by grace you have been saved through faith, and that not of yourselves; it is the gift of God, not of works, lest anyone should boast. For we are His workmanship, created in Christ Jesus for good works, which God prepared beforehand that we should walk in them.

The Lord Jesus Christ takes His rightful place on the Great White

---

[11] Philip Schaff, ed., *A Dictionary of the Bible: Including Biography, Natural History, Geography, Topography, Archeology, and Literature* (Philadelphia; New York; Chicago: American Sunday-School Union, 1880), 492.

Throne. The time is at the end of the world's existence, and no more births take place. God finished His redemptive plan, and He will destroy the present heavens and earth (2 Peter 3:10) and provide a new heaven and a new earth. The new heavens and earth will once again be in the original state that existed before sin entered the world (Revelation 21:1). God's final judicial act before entering the eternal state with all believers, is the sentencing of those who rejected His grace.

Revelation 20 deserves a closer examination to bring out the truths more definitively. The apostle John, the one who recorded the content of the book of Revelation as given to him directly from God (Revelation 1:1), provides prophetic or future information that God will fulfill exactly as recorded. Therefore, John states he saw the Great White Throne, which God will in fact fulfill literally in the future (Revelation 20:11). John further states that the person who sits on the throne is the all-powerful or omnipotent One "from whose face the earth and the heaven fled away. And there was found no place for them." (Revelation 20:11b) This passage once again indicates that God destroys the current earth and heavens immediately before the white throne judgment takes place.

Revelation 20:12 documents that all people--wealthy or poor, of great status or average--will stand at the judgment seat. The Judge is about to pronounce the eternal sentence, and all will stand in awe before their Creator, the Lord Jesus Christ. Where did these people come from? Revelation 20:13 states, "The sea gave up the dead who were in it, and Death and Hades delivered up the dead who were in them." Once again, it is imperative to remember that God previously resurrected all *believers* and placed them in heaven. Now the Lord is resurrecting all the unjust, defined as those who did not receive the gift of eternal life. The unjust are resurrected from their graves, and their soul and spirit from Hades, which is the place of the conscious dead until the Great White Throne judgment.

Now the Lord Jesus positions Himself on His Great White Throne, and each person will stand individually before the King of kings and Lord of lords. Jesus Christ opens the *Book of Life*, and their name is nowhere to be found. Jesus opens the books that contain their works, which will not in any shape, manner or form do anything but prove the absence of any positive works. (Revelation 12:12, 13) The Scriptures now confirm the choice that each defendant made during their lifetime. They never accepted the free gift of eternal life by faith, and now the books provide the unequivocal, undeniable facts. Jesus Christ has the entirety of the evidence in front of Him. The Lord Jesus now renders the irrevocable sentence as stated in Revelation 20:13-15.

> The sea gave up the dead who were in it, and Death and Hades delivered up the dead who were in them. And they were judged, each one according to his works. Then Death and Hades were cast into the lake of fire. This is the second death. And anyone not found written in the Book of Life was cast into the lake of fire.

Unbelievers are now cast into the Lake of Fire, the second, eternal death. You, the defendant, barring receiving the free gift of eternal life through what Jesus accomplished for you on the cross in His death, burial and resurrection, will suffer this intolerable sentence. God does not want this to happen to you. Therefore, the Lord has provided the evidence, the rule of law, and the exact jury instructions, and now He awaits your decision on what you will do.

Are you going to a better place or are you going to a much worse place after you take your last breath?

Please allow me the freedom to write in the first person. Regardless of whether we worked together, are strangers, acquaintances or friends, my heart's desire for you is that right now, if you have never placed your faith in Jesus Christ alone for eternal life that you receive that gift this very moment.

If you pulled a gun on me when I served as a deputy, if you threatened to kill me when I worked in the jail, if you disagreed with me in the courtroom, the boardroom, or the workplace, if you do or do not like me, please look beyond all of those things and please, please know that there is nothing more I want for you than for you to spend eternity in heaven with the Lord Jesus. Believe it or not, when we get to heaven, we will all live in unity.

May I please, one final time, invite you to stop, weigh the evidence provided, and take the free gift of eternal life that God wants to give you this very moment. Are you finally ready to reach out and accept God's sacrificial love and embrace His finished work on the cross including the Lord Jesus Christ's death, burial, and resurrection as full payment for your sins? If your answer is yes, then please do one thing, and thank the Lord Jesus for the eternal life He just guaranteed you when you placed your faith in Him. You can certainly talk to God in your own words as you would talk to any person you hold with high regard. If you are struggling for words, feel free to use the words that follow to help express your thankfulness to the Lord.

> Dear God, I fully understand that I am a sinner, and there is nothing good in me. I now understand that I do not deserve to go to heaven, but actually deserve eternal punishment. I am very thankful that Jesus Christ, Your Son, came down from heaven, was crucified, buried, and rose from the dead three days later to completely pay my sin debt. I receive the free gift of eternal life by placing my faith completely in what Jesus did for me. Thank you for saving me from my sins and the penalty for sin, and promising to take me to heaven when I die. In Jesus' name, Amen.

My heart rejoices if you received Christ as your personal Savior as a result of reading God's redemptive story in this book. I would love to help you begin your journey with the Lord Jesus. You can write me via email at:

Pastor.Rich@MyUGBC.com (or}

Rich@ProphecyFocusMinistries.com

or call (414) 788-6010 to let me know you recently received God's free gift of eternal life. Also, if you have questions or comments, please feel free to contact me.

Are YOU Going to a Better Place?

CHAPTER 6
Epilogue: Are Cops, Clergy, and Christians Compatible?

The question people ask me most often is how can a police officer also be involved in the ministry? The question itself is very telltale, as it reveals that the person has preconceived notions of what a police officer and a Christian should be. When one understands God's purpose for government, then one can easily reconcile what appears to be antithetical beliefs regarding the loving, peace-promoting Christian, and the tough, authoritative, armed officer. The Scriptures provide the documentation regarding why God Himself established the institution of government. Gaining Biblical insight into the three institutions that God formed provides clarity on why there should be no conflict between *cops*, Christians, and clergy.

In Genesis 1 and 2, God established the first institution, the family, which He specifically described in the following verse: "Therefore, a man shall leave his father and mother and be joined to his wife, and they shall become one flesh." (Genesis 2:24)

Genesis 3 describes the fall of humankind when Satan convinced Eve to disobey God. Eve subsequently convinced Adam, her husband, to make the conscious choice to disobey God. Adam's disobedience resulted in physical and spiritual death. Genesis 3—8 describes humankind's rebellion against God that resulted in God taking the lives of all but eight people--Noah, his wife, their 3 sons, and their wives. The world's population turned against God and chose a godless, corrupt, violent lifestyle.

> And the LORD was sorry that He had made man on the earth, and He was grieved in His heart. So the LORD said, "I will destroy man whom I have created from the face of the earth, both man and beast, creeping thing and birds of the air, for I am sorry that I have made them." But Noah found grace in the eyes of the LORD.
> (Genesis 6:6—8)

Moses records the reason for God's judgment via the catastrophic worldwide Flood that resulted in the massive loss of life.

The earth also was corrupt before God, and the earth was filled with violence. So God looked upon the earth, and indeed it was corrupt; for all flesh had corrupted their way on the earth. And God said to Noah, "The end of all flesh has come before Me, for the earth is filled with violence through them; and behold, I will destroy them with the earth." (Genesis 6:11–13)

Understanding what the Bible teaches is imperative for understanding why God formed human government. God's intention for humanity was that they love and care for one another. However, all of humanity rebelled against God, resulting in horrific hatred. Therefore, God brought punishment upon them in the form of a worldwide Flood. Carefully read the following passage.

Surely for your lifeblood I will demand a reckoning; from the hand of every beast I will require it, and from the hand of man. From the hand of every man's brother I will require the life of man. "Whoever sheds man's blood, By man his blood shall be shed; For in the image of God He made man." (Genesis 9:5-6)

God instituted human government to protect people from violence, and to hold criminals accountable for their actions.

The principle of Genesis 9:5-6, capital punishment, is widely debated among scholars, government officials, and the general public. God instituted capital punishment because humanity on a global scale chose to reject the concept of loving God and people, and instead turned to violence and murder. God mandated human government to protect the innocent from violence and murder. The Scriptures list the commandments God used to change the world filled with violence to a world where government and the rule of law, controlled violence, and held criminals accountable. In America, state and local governments have moved away from capital punishment, though it still exists in many states.

This book will not debate the topic of capital punishment and the historical changes. The purpose of broaching the topic is to show why God instituted human government, which is to protect people and hold offenders accountable.

Understanding the purpose of government, and the purpose of Christians and those in ministry should reveal no conflict in their outcomes. Police officers, who are government officials, swear an oath to serve and protect the people in their jurisdictions. God calls those who believe in Him to love and serve people, as outlined in Genesis 9. God called the clergy to serve, protect, and teach the Scriptures to all who will listen. When we analyze God's intentions for government, Christians, and the ministers of God's Word, we find they are synonymous.

When people questioned me about how I served in law enforcement as a Christian and a teacher of God's Word, I would usually respond with the following questions: Who do you want patrolling your streets and exercising leadership in your community? Do you want leadership and police with Biblical ethics and morality, who are taught to love, respect, and treat others with kindness, unless they are forced by a person's inappropriate conduct to use the minimal force necessary to stop the violation of the law? The answers to these questions should be obvious.

The Scriptures refer to those God calls into the ministry as shepherds and overseers of His people. The shepherd's purpose is never to beat down the sheep (a metaphor for God's people) but to protect them from violent attackers, and to provide them the necessities of life. Luke records God's charge to the ministers of His Word.

> Therefore, take heed to yourselves and to all the flock, among which the Holy Spirit has made you overseers, to shepherd the church of God which He purchased with His own blood.
> (Luke 20:28)

Many are familiar with Psalm 23 which beautifully describes the role of the Good Shepherd, Jesus Christ.

> The LORD is my shepherd; I shall not want. He makes me to lie down in green pastures; He leads me beside the still waters. He restores my soul; He leads me in the paths of righteousness For His name's sake. Yea, though I walk through the valley of the

shadow of death, I will fear no evil; For You are with me; Your rod and Your staff, they comfort me. You prepare a table before me in the presence of my enemies; You anoint my head with oil; My cup runs over. Surely goodness and mercy shall follow me All the days of my life; And I will dwell in the house of the LORD Forever. (Psalm 23:1-6)

The Psalm reveals that Jesus Christ, the great Shepherd, carries a rod and staff. The shepherd uses the staff to gently pull the wandering sheep back into the fold for their own protection. The shepherd also carried the rod, or club, wherewith the shepherd fought off those who attacked the sheep. Police perform the exact same tasks in helping and protecting the community where they serve. Helping people is the most common daily activity that police officers perform. They arrive at accidents and help the hurting. They respond to people in crisis who just experienced a horrific assault. The police exercise compassion when informing someone that their loved one has died. Police direct traffic, provide directions, and give lectures on public safety to children and adults. And yes, they rush into danger to stop those who choose to break the rule of law. Do police, clergy, and Christians have the same common goals of serving and protecting people? The answer is unequivocally, yes.

The most frustrating aspect of police work is when people come to the unfortunate conclusion that police are nothing more than legalized thugs. That perception, which is the result of a few less-than-respectable governmental leaders and officers wandering from the rule of law, is untenable. The key roles of clergy, Christians, and police officers are to serve and protect people by employing Biblical ethics, morality, and the rule of law as established by the legislature and enforced by the judicial system.

Who better to represent the community than police officers and clergy who adhere to the rule of law and Biblical standards? Scripture mandates that God's people adhere to the government's rule of law.

Let every soul be subject to the governing authorities. For there is no authority except from God, and the authorities that exist are appointed by God. Therefore, whoever resists the authority resists the ordinance of God, and those who resist will bring judgment on themselves. For rulers are not a terror to good works, but to evil. Do you want to be unafraid of the authority? Do what is good, and you will have praise from the same. For he is God's minister to you for good. But if you do evil, be afraid; for he does not bear the sword in vain; for he is God's minister, an avenger to execute wrath on him who practices evil. Therefore, you must be subject, not only because of wrath but also for conscience' sake. For because of this you also pay taxes, for they are God's ministers attending continually to this very thing. Render therefore to all their due: taxes to whom taxes are due, customs to whom customs, fear to whom fear, honor to whom honor. (Romans 13:1-7)

God clearly states that His people are not to be rebellious against those He places into governmental authority. The conditions that the Christians in Rome faced at the time Paul wrote this passage are astounding. The Christians suffered extreme persecution under the Roman government. Yet, God encouraged them not to rebel, but to submit to the government. Many theologians and Christians hotly debate the ramifications of that text; yet the principles of God's Word stand. God did not call His people to fight the government, but to focus on carrying out His mission.

The Scriptures, in multiple passages, reveal the mission of Jesus Christ.

For the Son of Man *Jesus Christ* has come to seek and to save that which was lost. (Luke 19:10)

This is a faithful saying and worthy of all acceptance, that Christ Jesus came into the world to save sinners, of whom I am chief. (1 Timothy 1:15)

God's mission is to reach people with the gospel, the good news that Jesus Christ entered the world to provide the only way for a person to get to heaven. Jesus Christ's purpose in coming to the earth was not to fight the government and overtake it. His mission, what He literally gave His life to accomplish, was to provide the pathway to heaven to all who would accept what He accomplished through His death, burial, and resurrection.

The Scriptures provide the mission for all who accept the free gift of salvation.

Now then, we are ambassadors for Christ, as though God were pleading through us: we implore you on Christ's behalf, be reconciled to God. (2 Corinthians 5:8)

The Scriptures define a true Christian as one who believed the gospel and received the free, unmerited gift of eternal life as outlined in Ephesians 2:8-9, "For by grace you have been saved through faith, and that not of yourselves; it is the gift of God, not of works, lest anyone should boast." God calls every true Christian to tell others how they can also have a personal relationship with Jesus Christ. In the process, God commands Christians to put off inappropriate or sinful behavior, and to live a Biblically compliant lifestyle for the Lord (Colossians 3:5-11). Are cops, Christians, and clergy compatible? The Scriptures point out the three callings are not only compatible, but that all three should be striving to achieve the same outcome.

God's Word reveals the third institution God formed. First, God instituted the family (Genesis 1-2). Second, God instituted human government (Genesis 9). Third, God instituted the church (Acts). The church is the institution He designed for His people to assemble, worship the Lord, hear God's Word, learn to share the gospel with others and send out missionaries around the world. The Bible contains many passages that describe the purpose of the church. The book of Acts describes the start of the New Testament church, which took place after the death, burial, and resurrection of Jesus Christ.

Many government agencies refer to churches as *faith-based organizations.* This politically correct name encompasses every possible religion in a community. Where does God want you to go, not only to learn more about Him, but to actively serve Him as well?

God's original design for the family, government, and the church was for these institutions to be dedicated to following His commands and principles. Society has corrupted all three institutions, and all three are suffering the consequences of what occurs when we violate God's Biblical principles. Most communities have many religious organizations and churches from which to choose. God formed the church to help people find Jesus Christ, and then to serve others by sharing the gospel in their community. Fewer churches are teaching the Bible than ever before, making it extremely difficult to find a Bible-believing church. People many times prefer a church that complies with their social and cultural norms over a true Bible-believing church that teaches the entire Word of God, and mandates accountability for inappropriate conduct.

What about you? Are you going to a better place, or a much worse place when you take your last breath? Is your answer to this question based upon verifiable, documented evidence, or are you trusting in speculation, circumstantial evidence, hearsay, or a manmade set of rules? You as the defendant, jury, and judge were called upon to carefully, and painstakingly, weigh the evidence, and determine your eternal destiny based on the facts, not speculation. It is decision time. What will you do with Jesus today? The Bible calls you to make the decision as quickly as possible, as today could be the day your take your last breath. Second Corinthians 6:2 calls you to determine your eternal destiny, "Behold, now is the accepted time; behold, now is the day of salvation." Would you please accept God's free gift of eternal life this very moment by placing your faith in what Jesus did for you in His death, burial, and resurrection?

> For by grace you have been saved through faith, and that not of yourselves; it is the gift of God, not of works, lest anyone should boast. (Ephesians 2:8–9)

Are you going to a better place when you take your last breath?

APPENDIX A
351 Old Testament Prophecies
Fulfilled in Jesus Christ's First Advent

Prophecy	Description	Fulfillment
1. Gen 3:15	Seed of a woman (virgin birth)	Gal 4:4-5; Matt 1:18
2. Gen 3:15	He will bruise Satan's head	Heb 2:14; 1 John 3:8
3. Gen 5:24	The bodily ascension to heaven illustrated	Mark 16:19
4. Gen 9:26-27	The God of Shem will be the Son of Shem	Luke 3:36
5. Gen 12:3	Seed of Abraham will bless all nations	Gal 3:8; Acts 3:25-26
6. Gen 12:7	The Promise made to Abraham's Seed	Gal 3:16
7. Gen 14:18	A priest after the order of Melchizedek	Heb 6:20
8. Gen 14:18	King of Peace and Righteousness	Heb 7:2
9. Gen 14:18	The Last Supper foreshadowed	Matt 26:26-29
10. Gen 17:19	Seed of Isaac (Gen 21:12)	Rom 9:7
11. Gen 22:8	The Lamb of God promised	John 1:29
12. Gen 22:18	As Isaac's seed, will bless all nations	Gal 3:16
13. Gen 26:2-5	The Seed of Isaac promised as the Redeemer	Heb 11:18
14. Gen 28:12	The Bridge to heaven	John 1:51

15. Gen 28:14	The Seed of Jacob	Luke 3:34
16. Gen 49:10	The time of His coming	Luke 2:1-7; Gal 4:4
17. Gen 49:10	The Seed of Judah	Luke 3:33
18. Gen 49:10	Called Shiloh or One Sent	John 17:3
19. Gen 49:10	Messiah to come before Judah lost identity	John 11:47-52
20. Gen 49:10	Unto Him shall the obedience of the people be	John 10:16
21. Ex 3:13-15	The Great "I AM"	John 4:26; 8:58
22. Ex 12:5	A Lamb without blemish	Heb 9:14; 1 Pet 1:19
23. Ex 12:13	The blood of the Lamb saves from wrath	Rom 5:8
24. Ex 12:21-27	Christ is our Passover	1 Cor 5:7
25. Ex 12:46	Not a bone of the Lamb to be broken	John 19:31-36
26. Ex 15:2	His exaltation predicted as Yeshua	Acts 7:55-56
27. Ex 15:11	His Character-Holiness	Luke 1:35; Acts 4:27
28. Ex 17:6	The Spiritual Rock of Israel	1 Cor 10:4
29. Ex 33:19	His Character-Merciful	Luke 1:72
30. Lev 1:2-9	His sacrifice a sweet smelling savor unto God	Eph 5:2
31. Lev 14:11	The leper cleansed-Sign to priesthood	Luke 5:12-14; Acts 6:7
32. Lev 16:15-17	Prefigures Christ's once-for-all death	Heb 9:7-14

33. Lev 16:27	Suffering outside the Camp	Matt 27:33; Heb. 13:11-12
34. Lev 17:11	The Blood-the life of the flesh	Matt 26:28; Mark 10:45
35. Lev 17:11	It is the blood that makes atonement	Rom. 3:23-24; 1 John 1:7
36. Lev 23:36-37	The Drink-offering: "If any man thirst"	John 7:37
37. Num 9:12	Not a bone of Him broken	John 19:31-36
38. Num 21:9	The serpent on a pole-Christ lifted up	John 3:14-18; 12:32
39. Num 24:17	Time: "I shall see him, but not now."	John 1:14; Gal 4:4
40. Deut 18:15	"This is of a truth that prophet"	John 6:14
41. Deut 18:15-16	"Had you believed Moses, you would believe me."	John 5:45-47
42. Deut 18:18	Sent by the Father to speak His word	John 8:28-29
43. Deut 18:19	Whoever will not hear must bear his sin	Acts 3:22-23
44. Deut 21:23	Cursed is he that hangs on a tree	Gal 3:10-13
45. Joshua 5:14-15	The Captain of our salvation	Heb 2:10
46. Ruth 4:4-10	Christ, our kinsman, has redeemed us	Eph 1:3-7
47. 1 Sam 2:35	A Faithful Priest	Heb. 2:17; 3:1-3, 6; 7:24-25
48. 1 Sam 2:10	Shall be an anointed King to the Lord	Matt 28:18; John 12:15

49. 2 Sam 7:12	David's Seed	Matt 1:1
50. 2 Sam 7:13	His Kingdom is everlasting	2 Pet 1:11
51. 2 Sam 7:14a	The Son of God	Luke 1:32; Rom 1:3-4
52. 2 Sam 7:16	David's house established forever	Luke 3:31; Rev 22:16
53. 2 Ki 2:11	The bodily ascension to heaven illustrated	Luke 24:51
54. 1 Chr 17:11	David's Seed	Matt 1:1; 9:27
55. 1 Chr 17:12-13	To reign on David's throne forever	Luke 1:32-33
56. 1 Chr 17:13	"I will be His Father, He...my Son."	Heb 1:5
57. Job 9:32-33	Mediator between man and God	1 Tim 2:5
58. Job 19:23-27	The Resurrection predicted	John 5:24-29
59. Psa 2:1-3	The enmity of kings foreordained	Acts 4:25-28
60. Psa 2:2	To own the title, Anointed (Christ)	John 1:41; Acts 2:36
61. Psa 2:6	His Character-Holiness	John 8:46; Rev 3:7
62. Psa 2:6	To own the title King	Matt 2:2
63. Psa 2:7	Declared the Beloved Son	Matt 3:17; Rom 1:4
64. Psa 2:7-8	The Crucifixion and Resurrection intimated	Acts 13:29-33
65. Psa 2:8-9	Rule the nations with a rod of iron	Rev 2:27; 12:5; 19:15
66. Psa 2:12	Life comes through faith in Him	John 20:31
67. Psa 8:2	The mouths of babes perfect	Matt 21:16

	His praise	
68. Psa 8:5-6	His humiliation and exaltation	Heb 2:5-9
69. Psa 9:7-10	Judge the world in righteousness	Acts 17:31
70. Psa 16:10	Was not to see corruption	Acts 2:31; 13:35
71. Psa 16:9-11	Was to arise from the dead	John 20:9
72. Psa 17:15	The resurrection predicted	Luke 24:6
73. Psa 18:2-3	The horn of salvation	Luke 1:69-71
74. Psa 22:1	Forsaken because of sins of others	2 Cor 5:21
75. Psa 22:1	"My God, my God, why have You forsaken me?"	Matt 27:46
76. Psa 22:2	Darkness upon Calvary for three hours	Matt 27:45
77. Psa 22:7	They shoot out the lip and shake the head	Matt 27:39-44
78. Psa 22:8	"He trusted in God, let Him deliver Him"	Matt 27:43
79. Psa 22:9-10	Born the Savior	Luke 2:7
80. Psa 22:12-13	They seek His death	John 19:6
81. Psa 22:14	His blood poured out when they pierced His side	John 19:34
82. Psa 22:14-15	Suffered agony on Calvary	Mark 15:34-37
83. Psa 22:15	He thirsted	John 19:28
84. Psa 22:16	They pierced His hands and His feet	John 19:34-37; 20:27
85. Psa 22:17-18	Stripped Him before the stares of men	Luke 23:34-35
86. Psa 22:18	They parted His garments	John 19:23-24

87. Psa 22:20-21	He committed Himself to God	Luke 23:46
88. Psa 22:20-21	Satanic power bruising the Redeemer's heel	Heb 2:14
89. Psa 22:22	His Resurrection declared	John 20:17
90. Psa 22:27-28	He shall be the governor of the nations	Col 1:16
91. Psa 22:31	"It is finished"	John 19:30; Heb 10:10-12, 14, 18
92. Psa 23:1	"I am the Good Shepherd"	John 10:11; 1 Pet 2:25
93. Psa 24:3	His exaltation predicted	Acts 1:11; Phil 2:9
94. Psa 30:3	His resurrection predicted	Acts 2:32
95. Psa 31:5	"Into Your hands I commit my spirit"	Luke 23:46
96. Psa 31:11	His acquaintances fled from Him	Mark 14:50
97. Psa 31:13	They took counsel to put Him to death	Matt 27:1; John 11:53
98. Psa 31:14-15	"He trusted in God, let Him deliver him"	Matt 27:43
99. Psa 34:20	Not a bone of Him broken	John 19:31-36
100. Psa 35:11	False witnesses rose up against Him	Matt 26:59
101. Psa 35:19	He was hated without a cause	John 15:25
102. Psa 38:11	His friends stood afar off	Luke 23:49
103. Psa 38:12	Enemies try to entangle Him by craft	Mark 14:1; Matt 22:15
104. Psa 38:12-13	Silent before His accusers	Matt 27:12-14
105. Psa 38:20	He went about doing good	Acts 10:38
106. Psa 40:2-5	The joy of His resurrection	John 20:20

		predicted	
107. Psa 40:6-8	His delight-the will of the Father		John 4:34; Heb 10:5-10
108. Psa 40:9	He was to preach the Righteousness in Israel		Matt 4:17
109. Psa 40:14	Confronted by adversaries in the Garden		John 18:4-6
110. Psa 41:9	Betrayed by a familiar friend		John 13:18
111. Psa 45:2	Words of Grace come from His lips		John 1:17; Luke 4:22
112. Psa 45:6	To own the title, God or Elohim		Heb 1:8
113. Psa 45:7	A special anointing by the Holy Spirit		Matt 3:16; Heb. 1:9
114. Psa 45:7-8	Called the Christ (Messiah or Anointed)		Luke 2:11
115. Psa 45:17	His name remembered forever		Eph 1:20-21; Heb. 1:8
116. Psa 55:12-14	Betrayed by a friend, not an enemy		John 13:18
117. Psa 55:15	Unrepentant death of the Betrayer		Matt 27:3-5; Acts 1:16-19
118. Psa 68:18	To give gifts to men		Eph 4:7-16
119. Psa 68:18	Ascended into Heaven		Luke 24:51
120. Psa 69:4	Hated without a cause		John 15:25
121. Psa 69:8	A stranger to own brethren		John 1:11; 7:5
122. Psa 69:9	Zealous for the Lord's House		John 2:17
123. Psa 69:14-20	Messiah's anguish of soul before crucifixion		Matt 26:36-45
124. Psa 69:20	"My soul is exceeding		Matt 26:38

	sorrowful"	
125. Psa 69:21	Given vinegar in thirst	Matt 27:34
126. Psa 69:26	The Savior given and smitten by God	John 17:4; 18:11
127. Psa 72:10-11	Great persons were to visit Him	Matt 2:1-11
128. Psa 72:16	The corn of wheat to fall into the Ground	John 12:24-25
129. Psa 72:17	Belief on His name will produce offspring	John 1:12-13
130. Psa 72:17	All nations shall be blessed by Him	Gal 3:8
131. Psa 72:17	All nations shall call Him blessed	John 12:13; Rev 5:8-12
132. Psa 78:1-2	He would teach in parables	Matt 13:34-35
133. Psa 78:2b	To speak the Wisdom of God with authority	Matt 7:29
134. Psa 80:17	The Man of God's right hand	Mark 14:61-62
135. Psa 88	The Suffering and Reproach of Calvary	Matt 27:26-50
136. Psa 88:8	They stood afar off and watched	Luke 23:49
137. Psa 89:27	Firstborn	Col 1:15-18
138. Psa 89:27	Emmanuel to be higher than earthly kings	Luke 1:32-33
139. Psa 89:35-37	David's Seed, throne, kingdom endure forever	Luke 1:32-33
140. Psa 89:36-37	His character-Faithfulness	Rev 1:5; 19:11
141. Psa 90:2	He is from everlasting (Micah 5:2)	John 1:1

142. Psa 91:11-12	Identified as Messianic, used to tempt Christ	Luke 4:10-11
143. Psa 97:9	His exaltation predicted	Acts 1:11; Eph 1:20
144. Psa 100:5	His character-Goodness	Matt 19:16-17
145. Psa 102:1-11	The Suffering and Reproach of Calvary	John 19:16-30
146. Psa 102:25-27	Messiah is the Preexistent Son	Heb 1:10-12
147. Psa 109:25	Ridiculed	Matt 27:39
148. Psa 110:1	Son of David	Matt 22:42-43
149. Psa 110:1	To ascend to the right-hand of the Father	Mark 16:19
150. Psa 110:1	David's son called Lord	Matt 22:44-45
151. Psa 110:4	A priest after Melchizedek's order	Heb 6:20
152. Psa 112:4	His character-Compassionate, Gracious, et al	Matt 9:36
153. Psa 118:17-18	Messiah's Resurrection assured	Luke 24:5-7; 1 Cor 15:20
154. Psa 118:22-23	The rejected stone is Head of the corner	Matt 21:42-43
155. Psa 118:26a	The Blessed One presented to Israel	Matt 21:9
156. Psa 118:26b	To come while Temple standing	Matt 21:12-15
157. Psa 132:11	The Seed of David (the fruit of His Body)	Luke 1:32; Act 2:30
158. Psa 129:3	He was scourged	Matt 27:26
159. Psa 138:1-6	The supremacy of David's Seed amazes kings	Matt 2:2-6

160. Psa 147:3-6	The earthly ministry of Christ described	Luke 4:18
161. Prov 1:23	He will send the Spirit of God	John 16:7
162. Prov 8:23	Foreordained from everlasting	Rev 13:8; 1 Pet 1:19-20
163. Song 5:16	The altogether lovely One	John 1:17
164. Isa 2:3	He shall teach all nations	John 4:25
165. Isa 2:4	He shall judge among the nations	John 5:22
166. Isa 6:1	When Isaiah saw His glory	John 12:40-41
167. Isa 6:8	The One Sent by God	John 12:38-45
168. Isa 6:9-10	Parables fall on deaf ears	Matt 13:13-15
169. Isa 6:9-12	Blinded to Christ and deaf to His words	Acts 28:23-29
170. Isa 7:14	To be born of a virgin	Luke 1:35
171. Isa 7:14	To be Emmanuel-God with us	Matt 1:18-23; 1 Tim 3:16
172. Isa 8:8	Called Emmanuel	Matt 28:20
173. Isa 8:14	A stone of stumbling, a Rock of offense	1 Pet 2:8
174. Isa 9:1-2	His ministry to begin in Galilee	Matt 4:12-17
175. Isa 9:6	A child born-Humanity	Luke 1:31
176. Isa 9:6	A Son given-Deity	Luke 1:32; John 1:14; 1 Tim 3:16
177. Isa 9:6	Declared to be the Son of God with power	Rom 1:3-4
178. Isa 9:6	The Wonderful One, Peleh	Luke 4:22
179. Isa 9:6	The Counselor, Yaatz	Matt 13:54
180. Isa 9:6	The Mighty God, El Gibor	1 Cor 1:24; Titus

		2:3
181. Isa 9:6	The Everlasting Father, Avi Adth	John 8:58; 10:30
182. Isa 9:6	The Prince of Peace, Sar Shalom	John 16:33
183. Isa 9:7	To establish an everlasting kingdom	Luke 1:32-33
184. Isa 9:7	His Character-Just	John 5:30
185. Isa 9:7	No end to his Government, Throne, and Peace	Luke 1:32-33
186. Isa 11:1	Called a Nazarene-the Branch, Netzer	Matt 2:23
187. Isa 11:1	A rod out of Jesse-Son of Jesse	Luke 3:23-32
188. Isa 11:2	Anointed One by the Spirit	Matt 3:16-17; Acts 10:38
189. Isa 11:2	His Character-Wisdom, Knowledge, et al	Col 2:3
190. Isa 11:3	He would know their thoughts	Luke 6:8; John 2:25
191. Isa 11:4	Judge in righteousness	Acts 17:31
192. Isa 11:4	Judges with the sword of His mouth	Rev 2:16; 19:11, 15
193. Isa 11:5	Character: Righteous & Faithful	Rev 19:11
194. Isa 11:10	The Gentiles seek Him	John 12:18-21
195. Isa 12:2	Called Jesus-Yeshua	Matt 1:21
196. Isa 22:22	The One given all authority to govern	Rev 3:7
197. Isa 25:8	The Resurrection predicted	1 Cor 15:54
198. Isa 26:19	His power of Resurrection predicted	Matt 27:50-54

199. Isa 28:16	The Messiah is the precious corner stone	Acts 4:11-12
200. Isa 28:16	The Sure Foundation	1 Cor 3:11; Matt 16:18
201. Isa 29:13	He indicated hypocritical obedience to His Word	Matt 15:7-9
202. Isa 29:14	The wise are confounded by the Word	1 Cor 1:18-31
203. Isa 32:2	A Refuge-A man shall be a hiding place	Matt 23:37
204. Isa 35:4	He will come and save you	Matt 1:21
205. Isa 35:5-6	To have a ministry of miracles	Matt 11:2-6
206. Isa 40:3-4	Preceded by forerunner	John 1:23
207. Isa 40:9	"Behold your God"	John 1:36; 19:14
208. Isa 40:10	He will come to reward	Rev 22:12
209. Isa 40:11	A shepherd-compassionate life-giver	John 10:10-18
210. Isa 42:1-4	The Servant-as a faithful, patient redeemer	Matt 12:18-21
211. Isa 42:2	Meek and lowly	Matt 11:28-30
212. Isa 42:3	He brings hope for the hopeless	John 4
213. Isa 42:4	The nations shall wait on His teachings	John 12:20-26
214. Isa 42:6	The Light (salvation) of the Gentiles	Luke 2:32
215. Isa 42:1-6	His is a worldwide compassion	Matt 28:19-20
216. Isa 42:7	Blind eyes opened	John 9:25-38
217. Isa 43:11	He is the only Savior	Acts 4:12
218. Isa 44:3	He will send the Spirit of God	John 16:7-13

219. Isa 45:21-25	He is Lord and Savior	Phil 3:20; Titus 2:13
220. Isa 45:23	He will be the Judge	John 5:22; Rom 14:11
221. Isa 46:9-10	Declares things not done	John 13:19
222. Isa 48:12	The First and the Last	John 1:30; Rev 1:8, 17
223. Isa 48:16-17	He came as a Teacher	John 3:2
224. Isa 49:1	Called from the womb-His humanity	Matt 1:18
225. Isa 49:5	A Servant from the womb	Luke 1:31; Phil 2:7
226. Isa 49:6	He will restore Israel	Acts 3:19-21; 15:16-17
227. Isa 49:6	He is Salvation for Israel	Luke 2:29-32
228. Isa 49:6	He is the Light of the Gentiles	John 8:12; Acts 13:47
229. Isa 49:6	He is Salvation unto the ends of the earth	Acts 15:7-18
230. Isa 49:7	He is despised of the Nation	John 1:11; 8:48-49; 19:14-15
231. Isa 50:3	Heaven is clothed in black at His humiliation	Luke 23:44-45
232. Isa 50:4	He is a learned counselor for the weary	Matt 7:29; 11:28-29
233. Isa 50:5	The Servant bound willingly to obedience	Matt 26:39
234. Isa 50:6a	"I gave my back to those who struck Me"	Matt 27:26
235. Isa 50:6b	He was smitten on the cheeks	Matt 26:67
236. Isa 50:6c	He was spat upon	Matt 27:30

237. Isa 52:7	Published good tidings upon mountains	Matt 5:12; 15:29; 28:16
238. Isa 52:13	The Servant exalted	Acts 1:8-11; Eph 1:19-22; Phil 2:5-9
239. Isa 52:14	The Servant shockingly abused	Luke 18:31-34; Matt 26:67-68
240. Isa 52:15	Nations startled by message of the Servant	Luke 18:31-34; Matt 26:67-68
241. Isa 52:15	His blood shed sprinkles nations	Heb 9:13-14; Rev 1:5
242. Isa 53:1	His people would not believe Him	John 12:37-38
243. Isa 53:2	Appearance of an ordinary man	Phil 2:6-8
244. Isa 53:3a	Despised	Luke 4:28-29
245. Isa 53:3b	Rejected	Matt 27:21-23
246. Isa 53:3c	Great sorrow and grief	Matt 26:37-38; Luke 19:41; Heb 4:15
247. Isa 53:3d	Men hide from being associated with Him	Mark 14:50-52
248. Isa 53:4a	He would have a healing ministry	Matt 8:16-17
249. Isa 53:4b	Thought to be cursed by God	Matt 26:66; 27:41-43
250. Isa 53:5a	Bears penalty for mankind's iniquities	2 Cor 5:21; Heb 2:9
251. Isa 53:5b	His sacrifice provides peace between man and God	Col 1:20
252. Isa 53:5c	His sacrifice would heal man of sin	1 Pet 2:24
253. Isa 53:6a	He would be the sin-bearer	1 John 2:2; 4:10

		for all mankind	
254. Isa 53:6b		God's will that He bear sin for all mankind	Gal 1:4
255. Isa 53:7a		Oppressed and afflicted	Matt 27:27-31
256. Isa 53:7b		Silent before his accusers	Matt 27:12-14
257. Isa 53:7c		Sacrificial lamb	John 1:29; 1 Pet 1:18-19
258. Isa 53:8a		Confined and persecuted	Matt 26:47-27:31
259. Isa 53:8b		He would be judged	John 18:13-22
260. Isa 53:8c		Killed	Matt 27:35
261. Isa 53:8d		Dies for the sins of the world	1 John 2:2
262. Isa 53:9a		Buried in a rich man's grave	Matt 27:57
263. Isa 53:9b		Innocent and had done no violence	Luke 23:41; John 18:38
264. Isa 53:9c		No deceit in his mouth	1 Pet 2:22
265. Isa 53:10a		God's will that He die for man	John 18:11
266. Isa 53:10b		An offering for sin	Matt 20:28; Gal 3:13
267. Isa 53:10c		Resurrected and live forever	Rom 6:9
268. Isa 53:10d		He would prosper	John 17:1-5
269. Isa 53:11a		God fully satisfied with His suffering	John 12:27
270. Isa 53:11b		God's servant would justify man	Rom 5:8-9, 18-19
271. Isa 53:11c		The sin-bearer for all mankind	Heb 9:28
272. Isa 53:12a		Exalted by God because of his sacrifice	Matt 28:18
273. Isa 53:12b		He would give up his life to save mankind	Luke 23:46

274. Isa 53:12c	Numbered with the transgressors	Mark 15:27-28
275. Isa 53:12d	Sin-bearer for all mankind	1 Pet 2:24
276. Isa 53:12e	Intercede to God in behalf of mankind	Luke 23:34; Rom 8:34
277. Isa 55:3	Resurrected by God	Acts 13:34
278. Isa 55:4a	A witness	John 18:37
279. Isa 55:4b	He is a leader and commander	Heb 2:10
280. Isa 55:5	God would glorify Him	Acts 3:13
281. Isa 59:16a	Intercessor between man and God	Matt 10:32
282. Isa 59:16b	He would come to provide salvation	John 6:40
283. Isa 59:20	He would come to Zion as their Redeemer	Luke 2:38
284. Isa 60:1-3	He would show light to the Gentiles	Acts 26:23
285. Isa 61:1a	The Spirit of God upon him	Matt 3:16-17
286. Isa 61:1b	The Messiah would preach the good news	Luke 4:16-21
287. Isa 61:1c	Provide freedom from the bondage of sin	John 8:31-36
288. Isa 61:1-2a	Proclaim a period of grace	Gal 4:4-5
289. Jer 23:5-6	Descendant of David	Luke 3:23-31
290. Jer 23:5-6	The Messiah would be both God and Man	John 13:13; 1 Tim 3:16
291. Jer 31:22	Born of a virgin	Matt 1:18-20
292. Jer 31:31	The Messiah would be the new covenant	Matt 26:28
293. Jer 33:14-15	Descendant of David	Luke 3:23-31

294. Ezek 34:23-24	Descendant of David	Matt 1:1
295. Ezek 37:24-25	Descendant of David	Luke 1:31-33
296. Dan 2:44-45	The Stone that shall break the kingdoms	Matt 21:44
297. Dan 7:13-14a	He would ascend into heaven	Acts 1:9-11
298. Dan 7:13-14b	Highly exalted	Eph 1:20-22
299. Dan 7:13-14c	His dominion would be everlasting	Luke 1:31-33
300. Dan 9:24a	To make an end to sins	Gal 1:3-5
301. Dan 9:24a	To make reconciliation for iniquity	Rom 5:10; 2 Cor 5:18-21
302. Dan 9:24b	He would be holy	Luke 1:35
303. Dan 9:25	His announcement	John 12:12-13
304. Dan 9:26a	Cut off	Matt 16:21; 21:38-39
305. Dan 9:26b	Die for the sins of the world	Heb 2:9
306. Dan 9:26c	Killed before the destruction of the temple	Matt 27:50-51
307. Dan 10:5-6	Messiah in a glorified state	Rev 1:13-16
308. Hos 11:1	He would be called out of Egypt	Matt 2:15
309. Hos 13:14	He would defeat death	1 Cor 15:55-57
310. Joel 2:32	Offer salvation to all mankind	Rom 10:9-13
311. Jonah 1:17	Death and resurrection of Christ	Matt 12:40; 16:4
312. Mic 5:2a	Born in Bethlehem	Matt 2:1-6

313. Mic 5:2b	Ruler in Israel	Luke 1:33
314. Mic 5:2c	From everlasting	John 8:58
315. Hag 2:6-9	He would visit the second Temple	Luke 2:27-32
316. Hag 2:23	Descendant of Zerubbabel	Luke 2:27-32
317. Zech 3:8	God's servant	John 17:4
318. Zech 6:12-13	Priest and King	Heb 8:1
319. Zech 9:9a	Greeted with rejoicing in Jerusalem	Matt 21:8-10
320. Zech 9:9b	Beheld as King	John 12:12-13
321. Zech 9:9c	The Messiah would be just	John 5:30
322. Zech 9:9d	The Messiah would bring salvation	Luke 19:10
323. Zech 9:9e	The Messiah would be humble	Matt 11:29
324. Zech 9:9f	Presented to Jerusalem riding on a donkey	Matt 21:6-9
325. Zech 10:4	The cornerstone	Eph 2:20
326. Zech 11:4-6a	At His coming, Israel to have unfit leaders	Matt 23:1-4
327. Zech 11:4-6b	Rejection causes God to remove His protection	Luke 19:41-44
328. Zech 11:4-6c	Rejected in favor of another king	John 19:13-15
329. Zech 11:7	Ministry to "poor," the believing remnant	Matt 9:35-36
330. Zech 11:8a	Unbelief forces Messiah to reject them	Matt 23:33
331. Zech 11:8b	Despised	Matt 27:20
332. Zech 11:9	Stops ministering to those who rejected Him	Matt 13:10-11

333. Zech 11:10-11a	Rejection causes God to remove protection	Luke 19:41-44
334. Zech 11:10-11b	The Messiah would be God	John 14:7
335. Zech 11:12-13a	Betrayed for thirty pieces of silver	Matt 26:14-15
336. Zech 11:12-13b	Rejected	Matt 26:14-15
337. Zech 11:12-13c	Thirty pieces of silver cast in the house of the Lord	Matt 27:3-5
338. Zech 11:12-13d	The Messiah would be God	John 12:45
339. Zech 12:10a	The Messiah's body would be pierced	John 19:34-37
340. Zech 12:10b	The Messiah would be both God and man	John 10:30
341. Zech 12:10c	The Messiah would be rejected	John 1:11
342. Zech 13:7a	God's will He die for mankind	John 18:11
343. Zech 13:7b	A violent death	Mark 14:27
344. Zech 13:7c	Both God and man	John 14:9
345. Zech 13:7d	Israel scattered as a result of rejecting Him	Matt 26:31-56
346. Zech 14:4	He would return to the Mt. of Olives	Acts 1:11-12
347. Mal 3:1a	Messenger to prepare the way for Messiah	Mark 1:1-8
348. Mal 3:1b	Sudden appearance at the temple	Mark 11:15-16
349. Mal 3:1c	Messenger of the new covenant	Luke 4:43

| 350. Mal 4:5 | Forerunner in spirit of Elijah | Matt 3:1-3; 11:10-14; 17:11-13 |
| 351. Mal 4:6 | Forerunner would turn many to righteousness | Luke 1:16-17 |

APPENDIX B
RESOURCES FOR FURTHER CONSIDERATION

J.B. Hixson, *Getting the Gospel Wrong* (Duluth, MN.: Grace Gospel Press) 2013.

John F. Walvoord, *Every Prophecy of the Bible* (Colorado Springs, CO.: David C. Cook) 2011.

Josh McDowell, *The New Evidence that Demands a Verdict* (Nashville TN.: Thomas Nelson, Inc) 1999.

Lorna Simcox, *The Search* (Bellmawr, NJ.: The Friends of Israel Gospel Ministry, Inc.) 2

Mark Hitchcock, *The End* (Carol Stream, ILL.: Tyndale House Publishers, Inc.) 2012.

Paul E. Little, *Know Why You Believe* (Westmont, IL: IVP Books, 2008).

Roy B. Zuck, *Basic Bible Interpretation* (Colorado Springs, CO.: David C. Cook) 1991.

The Bible Knowledge Commentary: An Exposition of the Scriptures, General Editors J. F. Walvoord and R. B. Zuck, vol. 1 (Wheaton, IL: Victor Books) 1985

Are YOU Going to a Better Place?

ABOUT THE AUTHOR

Richard R. Schmidt, D.Min., and Ph.D. has been an avid student of the Word of God for over 43 years. Dr. and Mrs. Schmidt have been married 41 years, have three married children & nine grandchildren.

Rich brings with him an extremely unique and diverse background. After giving his life to Christ during a Chicago revival meeting, he immediately immersed himself into evangelism and the study of Scripture, graduating with both a B.S. and M.A. in Pastoral Theology/Christian Education. Early in his ministry, Rich traveled with Evangelist Joe Boyd and preached in various churches and venues, including Chicago's Pacific Garden Mission. Upon college graduation and ordination, Rich and his wife, Valori, moved to Milwaukee, WI to church plant.

After the church plant was successfully merged with another, Rich joined the Milwaukee County Sheriff's Office to support his young family, while simultaneously serving as an Assistant Pastor. During the next 18 years, he regularly preached, taught Bible classes, and led the Men's Ministry. Rich was also rising to the top of the MCSO. At MCSO, he received extensive training in Leadership and Administration at the FBI Academy, Harvard & Northwestern Universities, and the National Institute of Corrections.

On September 1, 2017, upon the retirement of the Sheriff, Rich became the Acting Sheriff of Milwaukee County, WI until his retirement in January, 2019. During that time, Rich transformed the agency with 18 initiatives and maintained positive working relationships with County & State government leaders.

It was during his combined government and ministry period that Rich met Dr. Jimmy DeYoung, Dr. Bob Shelton, and traveled with Dr. Sam Horn on multiple study trips to the Middle East. From those encounters, a passion for Israel and its Biblical history and prophetic significance emerged. In 2014, after completing a prophetically based doctoral program, Rich was awarded his D.Min., and **Prophecy Focus Ministries** was born. In 2020, Rich earned his Ph.D. in Advanced Eschatology and continued his robust speaking schedule.

From 2017-2020, Rich was a volunteer church representative with the Friends of Israel Gospel Ministry. He co-led study trips to Israel and preached at multiple FOI local and national Prophecy Conferences, along with co-authoring a book with FOI. His love for the Jewish people continues to this day.

In 2020, the Covid pandemic with its widespread cancellations allowed Rich to speak at Union Grove Baptist Church. Within a short time, the call to become the Senior Pastor at UGBC was extended to Dr. and Mrs. Schmidt. Additionally, Rich began a weekly televised program, *Prophecy Focus*, which can be viewed on VCY, Ch 30 and VCY.TV. He also is a featured speaker at Prophecy Conferences when not preaching at UGBC.

Rich combines an evangelistic flavor with Scripturally packed, exciting messages that are visualized with detailed multi-media presentations. Dr. Schmidt is able to marry that with his up-to-date knowledge of current events and experience that has been gained during his thirty-two years in a large government agency.

BOOKS BY DR. RICHARD SCHMIDT

Daniel's Gap Paul's Mystery, What Paused the Prophetic Calendar, Hales Corners, WI.: Prophecy Focus Ministries, Inc., 2016.

Tribulation to Triumph, Hales Corners, WI.: Prophecy Focus Ministries, Inc., 2019.

Co-Authored: *Thy Kingdom Come*, Jim Showers & Chris Katulka General Editors, Bellmawr, NJ.: The Friends of Israel Gospel Ministry, Inc., 2019.

Are You Going to a Better Place?, Hales Corners, WI.: Prophecy Focus Ministries, Inc., 2022.

WEB SITES
Prophecy Focus Ministries: ProphecyFocus.org
Union Grove Baptist Church: MyUGBC.com

EMAIL ADDRESSES
Rich@ProphecyFocusMinistries.com
Pastor.Rich@MyUGBC.com

TEXT OR CALL
(414) 788-6010

Made in the USA
Middletown, DE
17 May 2022

65863529R00053